MW01268937

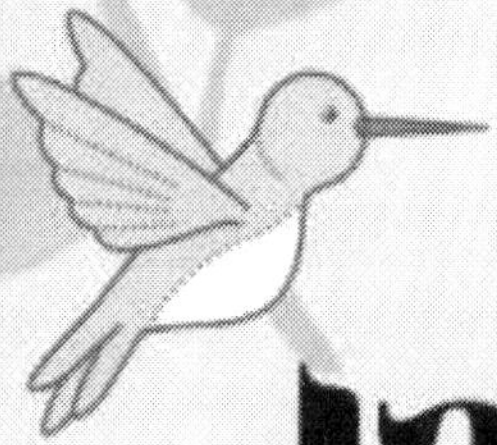

large print humming bird coloring book for adult

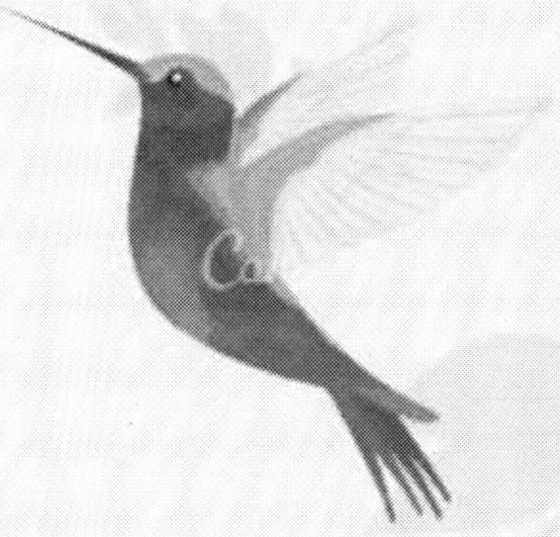

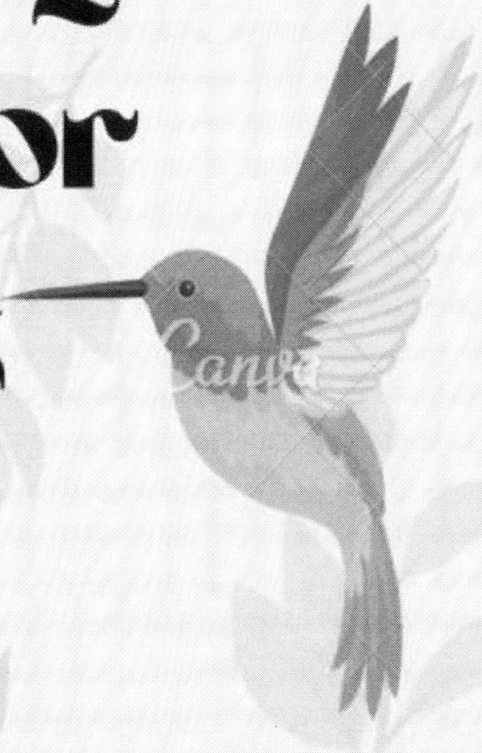

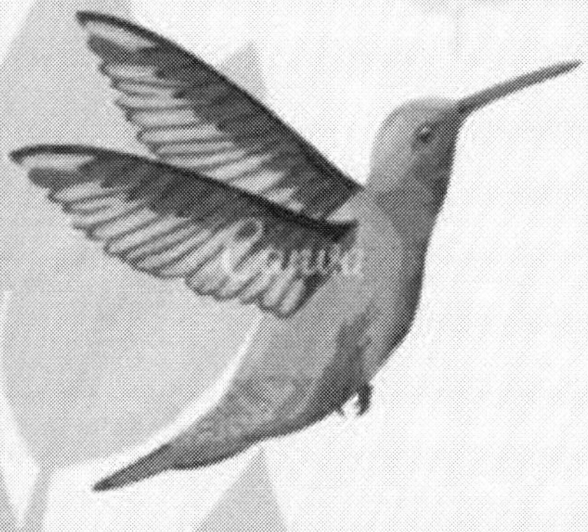

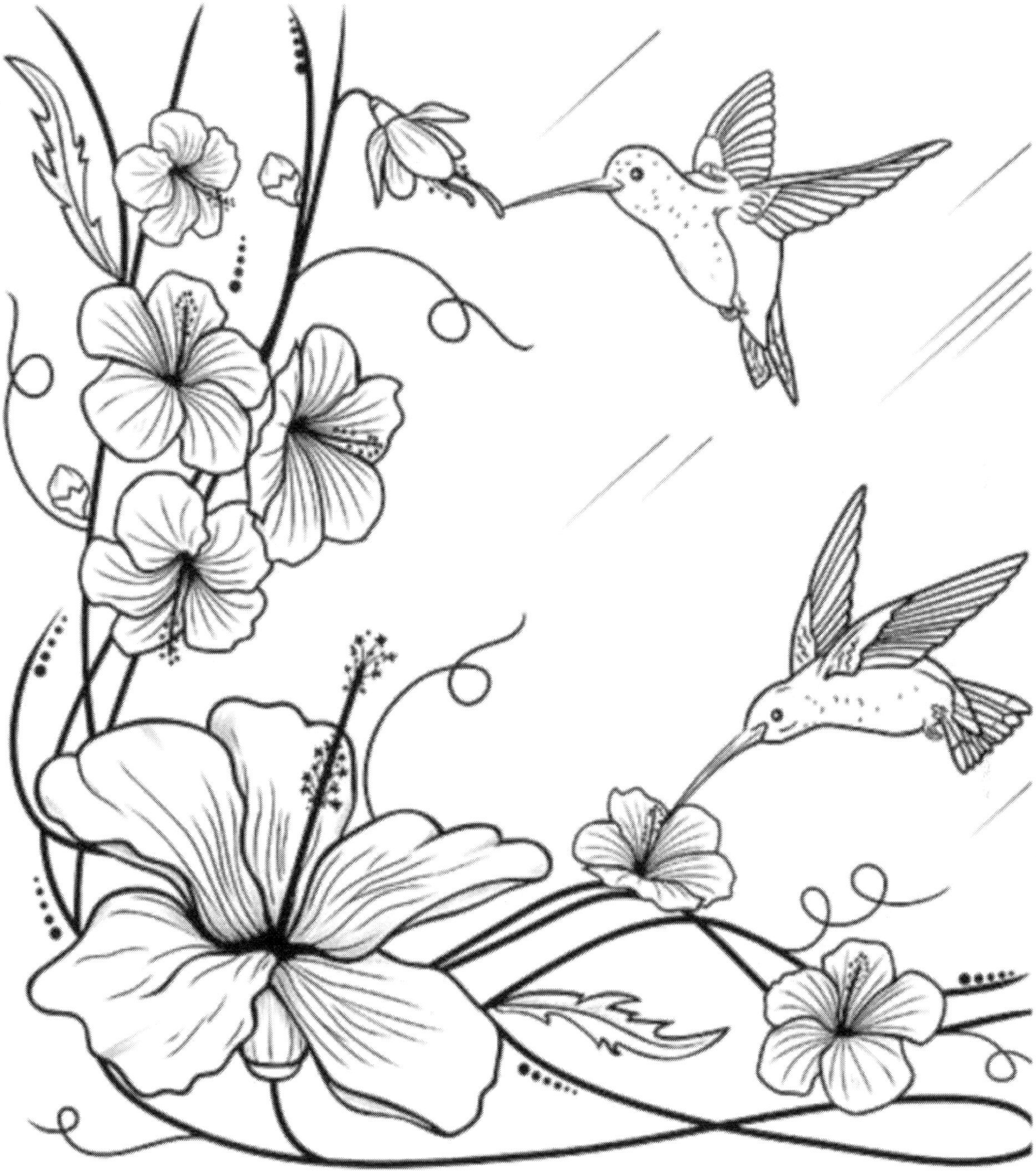

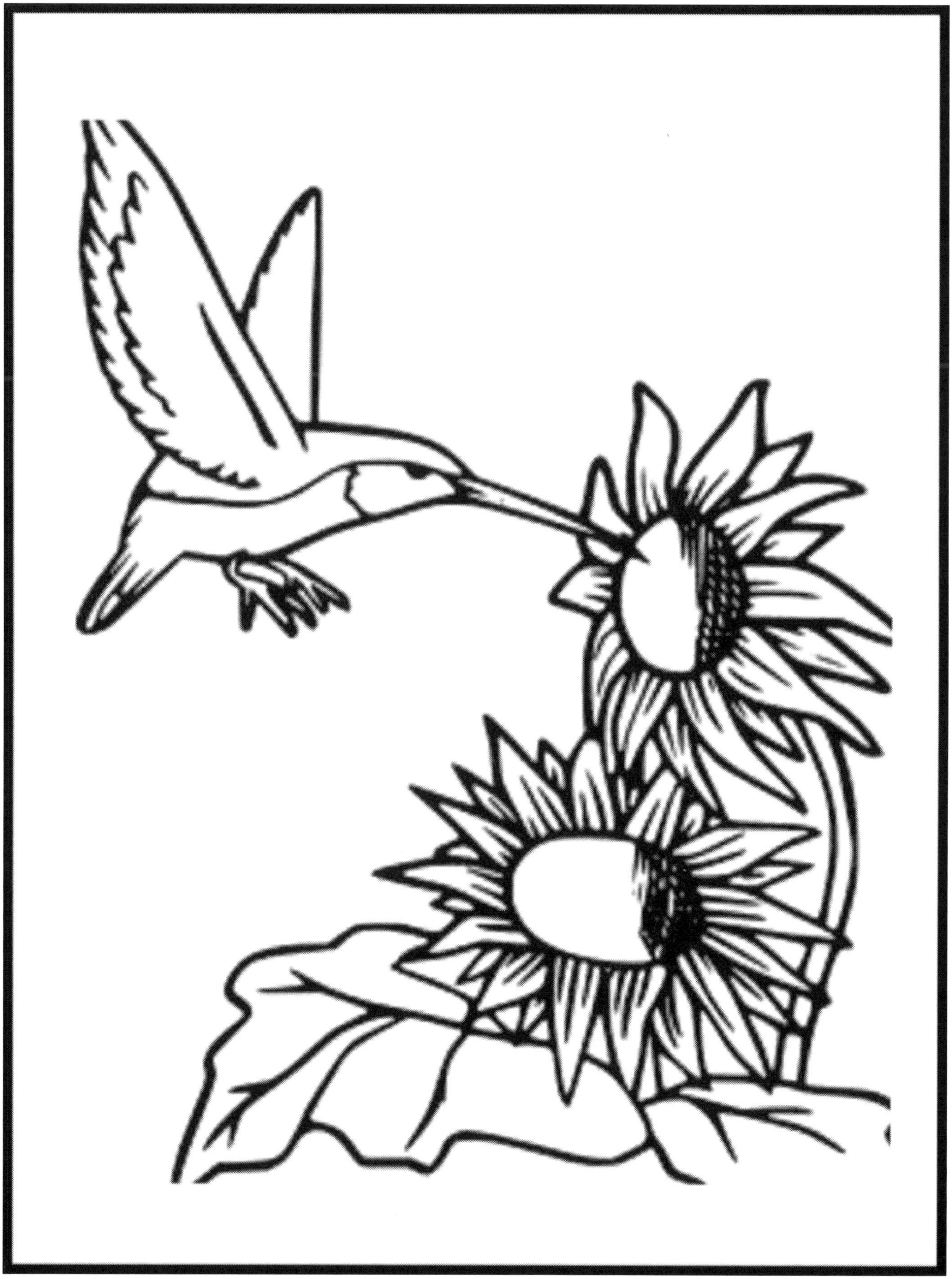

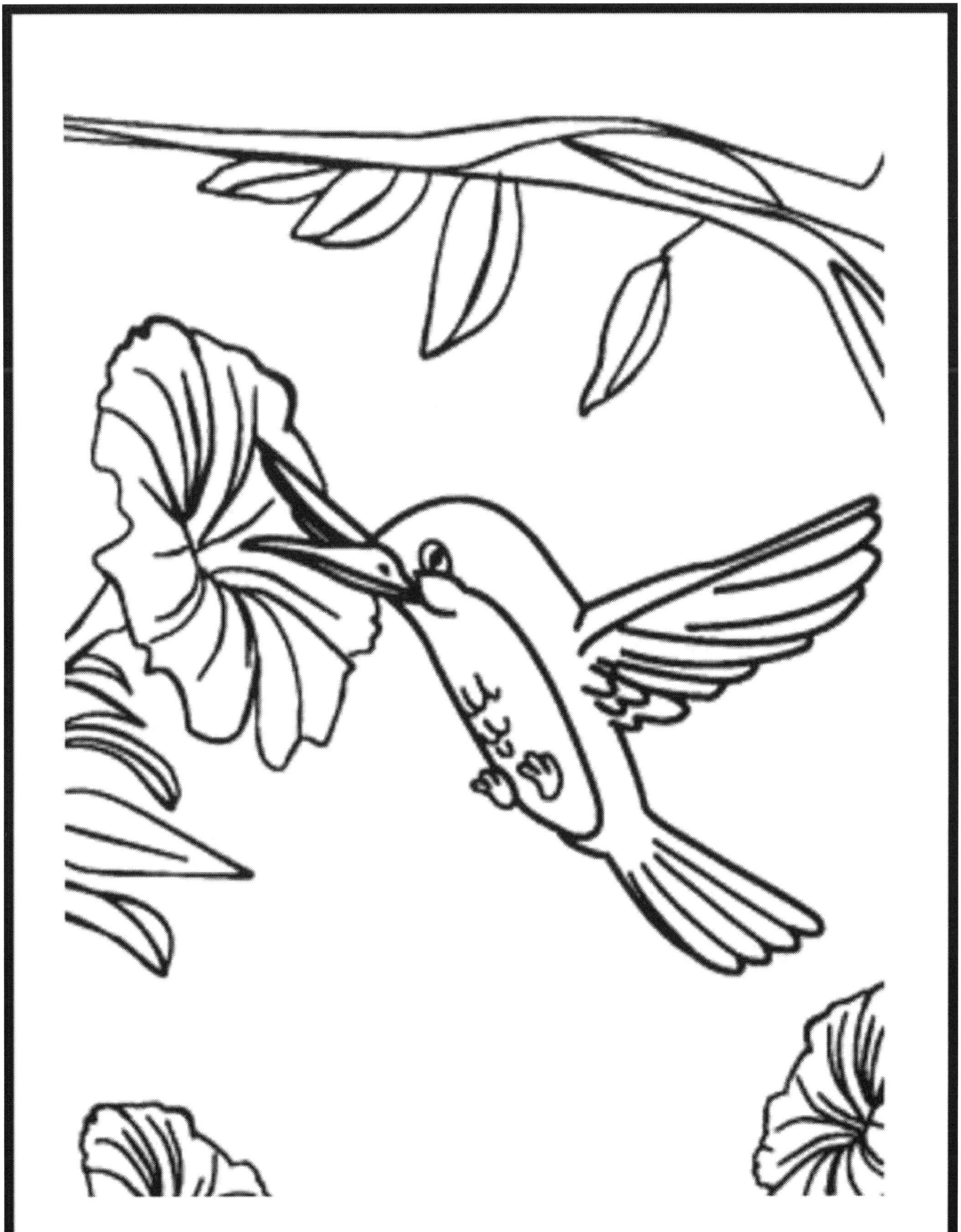

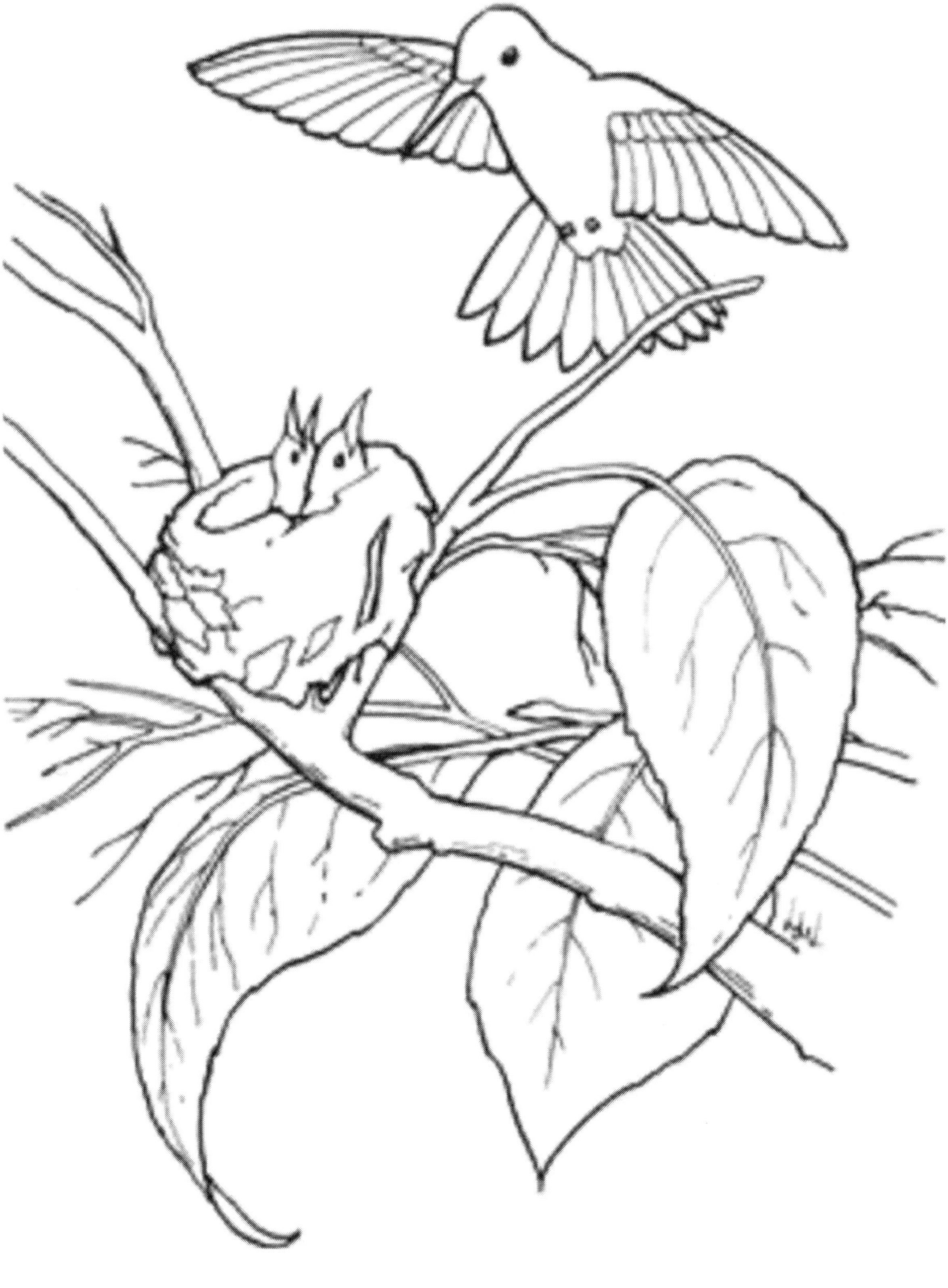

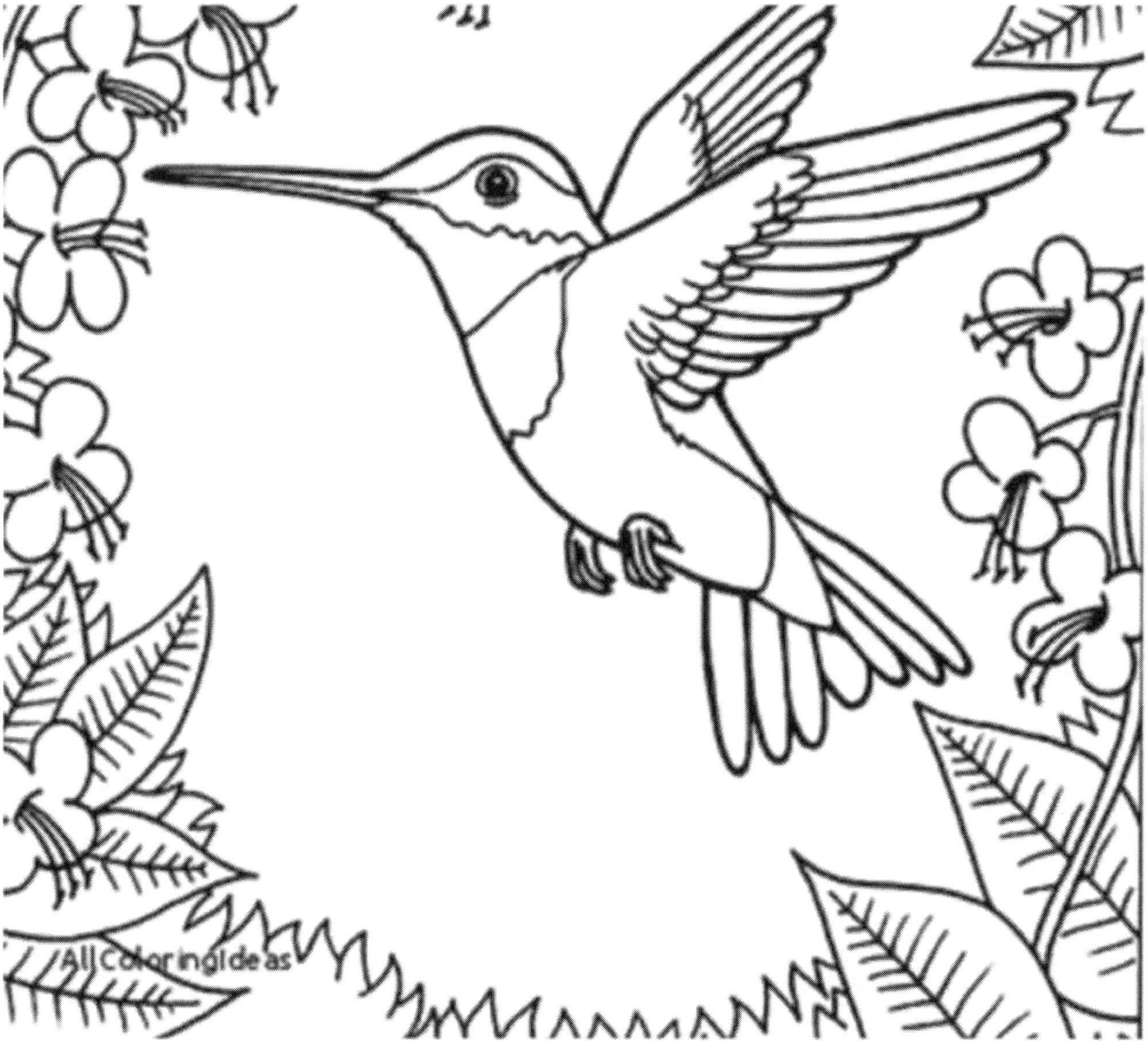
AllColoringIdeas

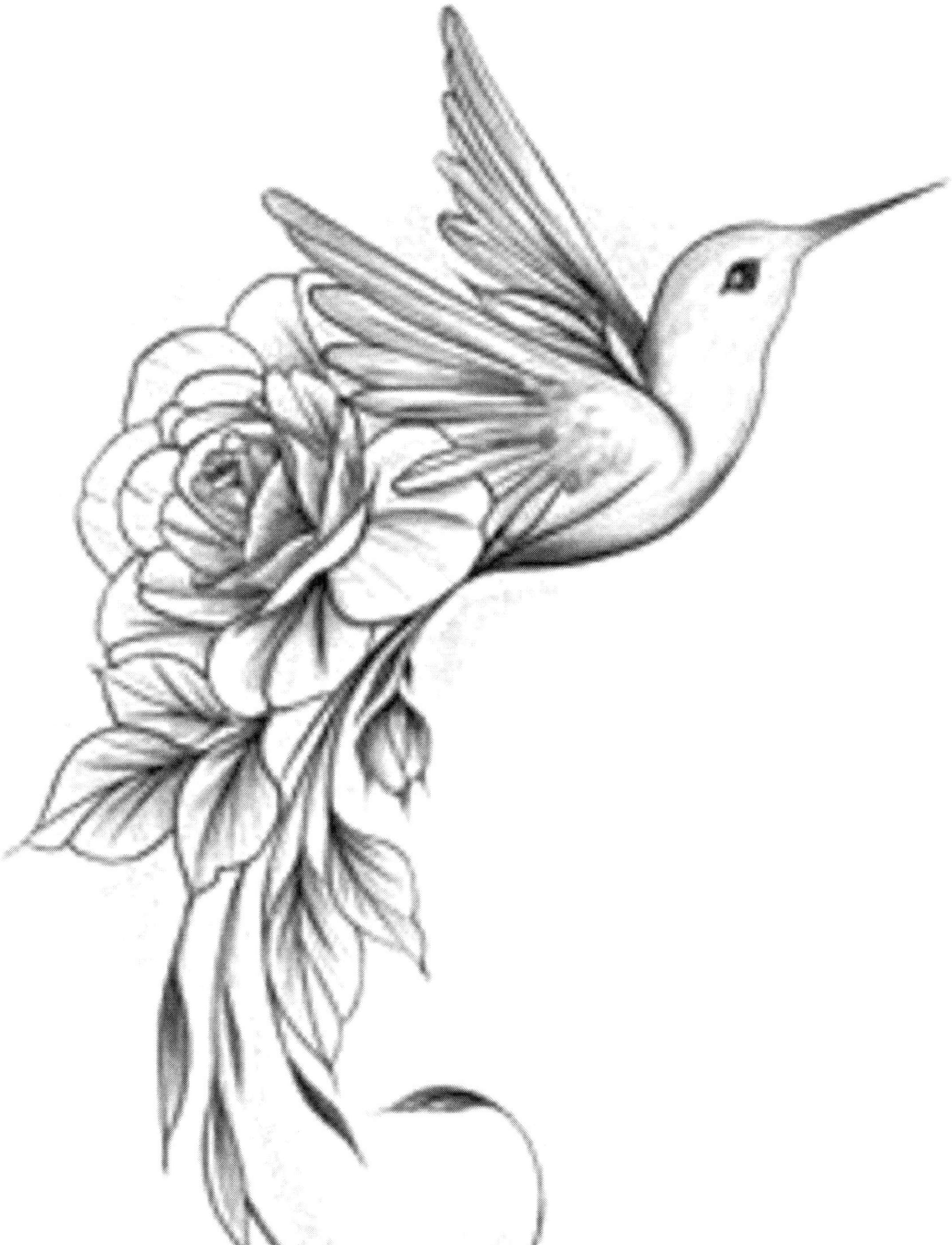

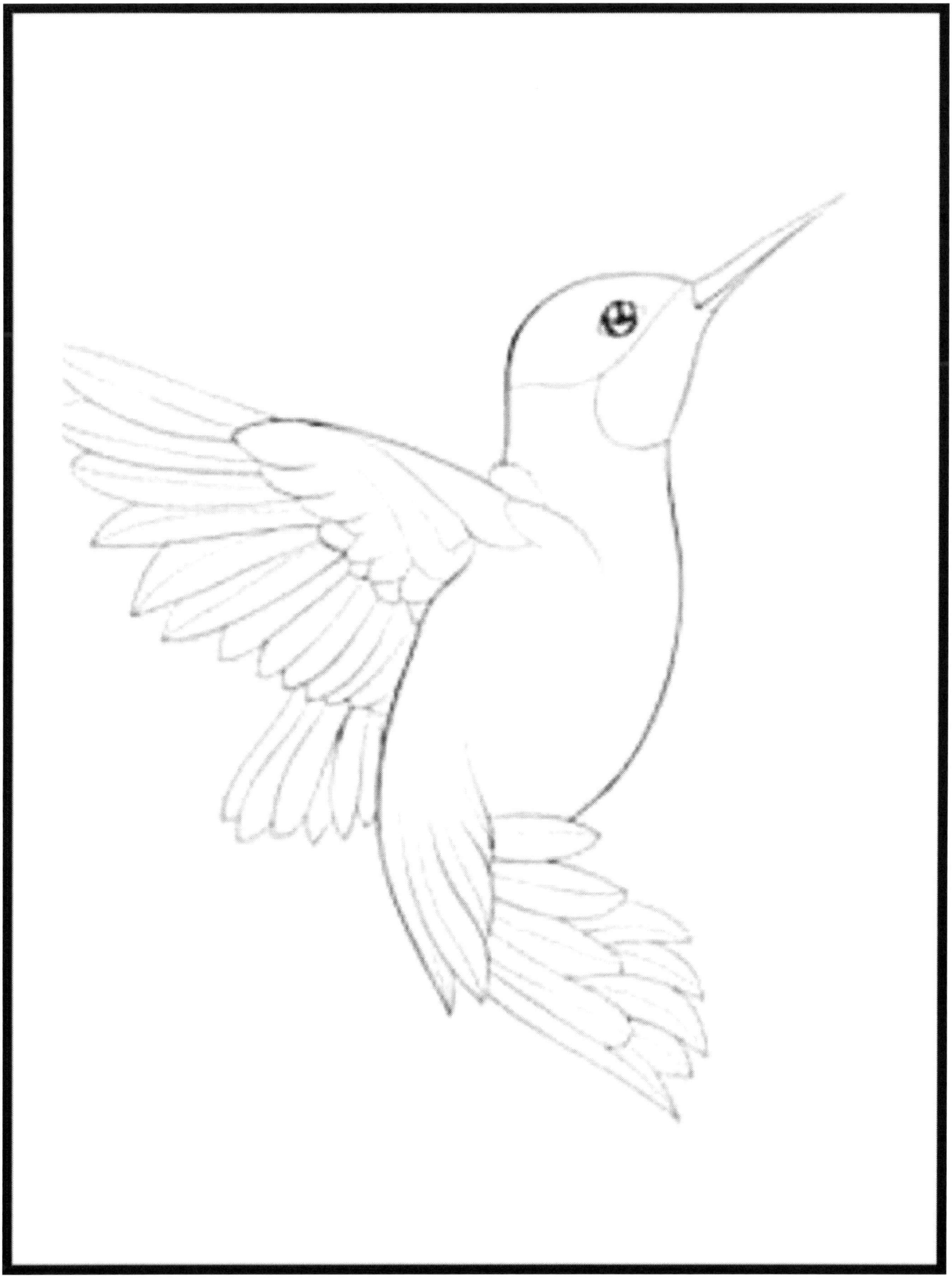

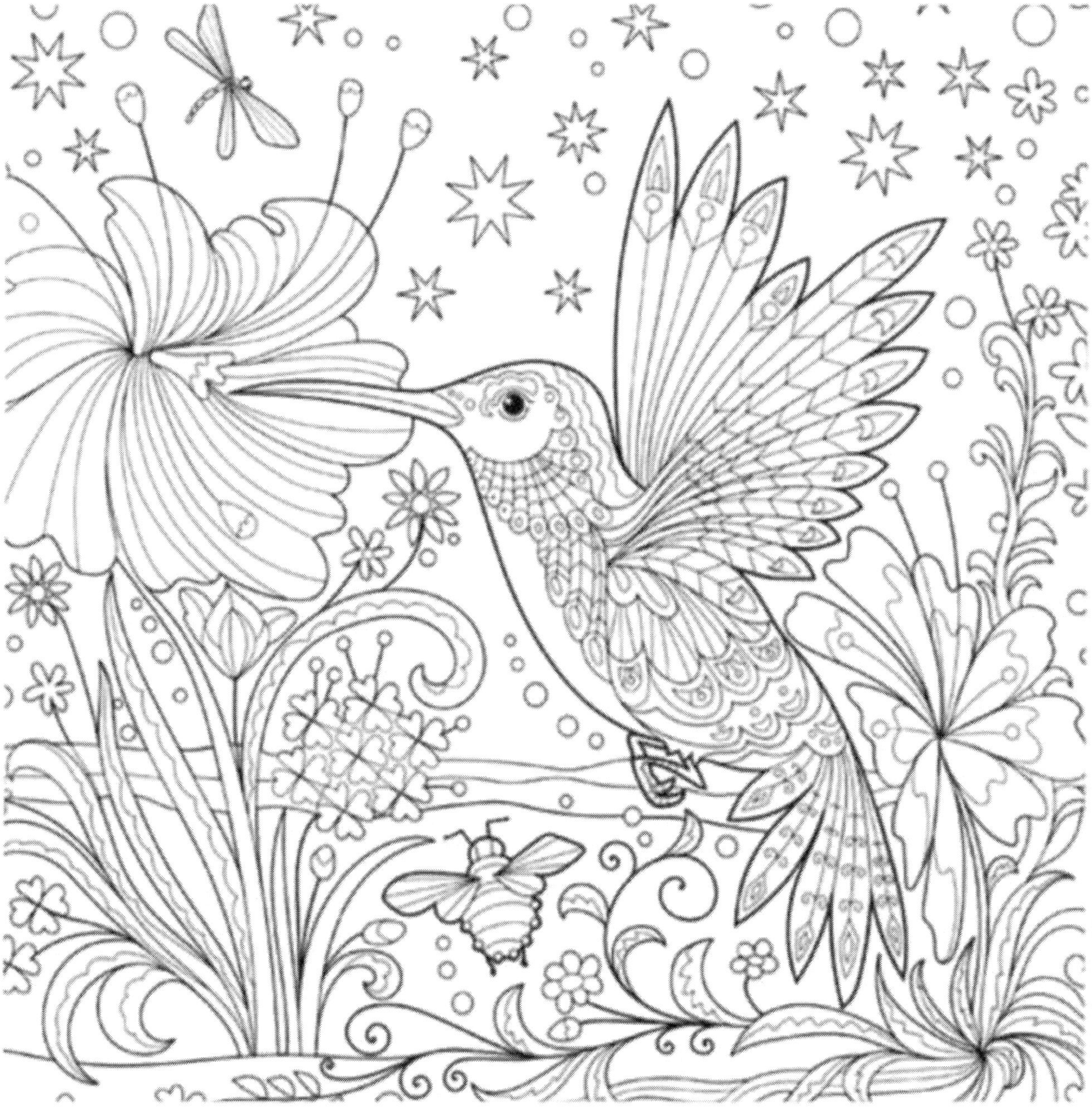

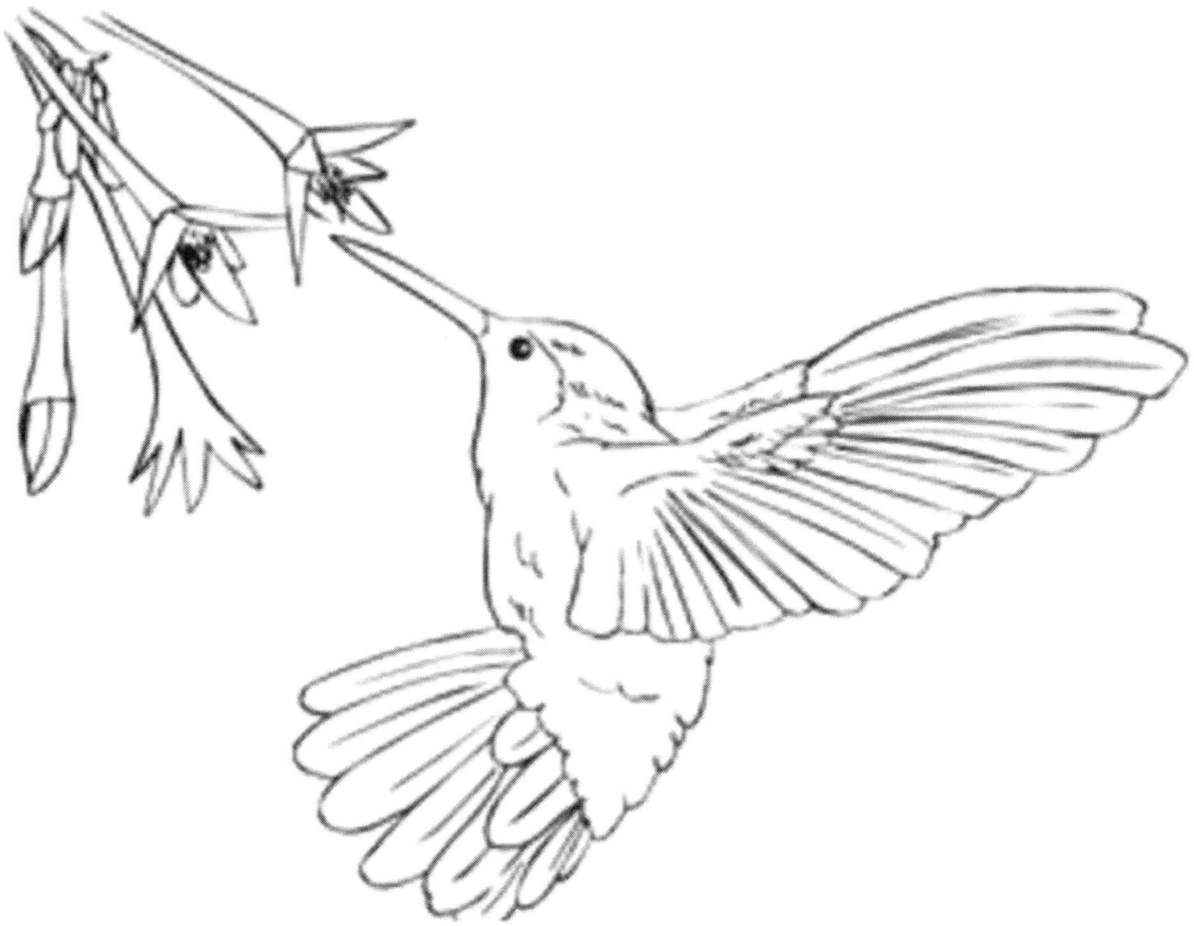

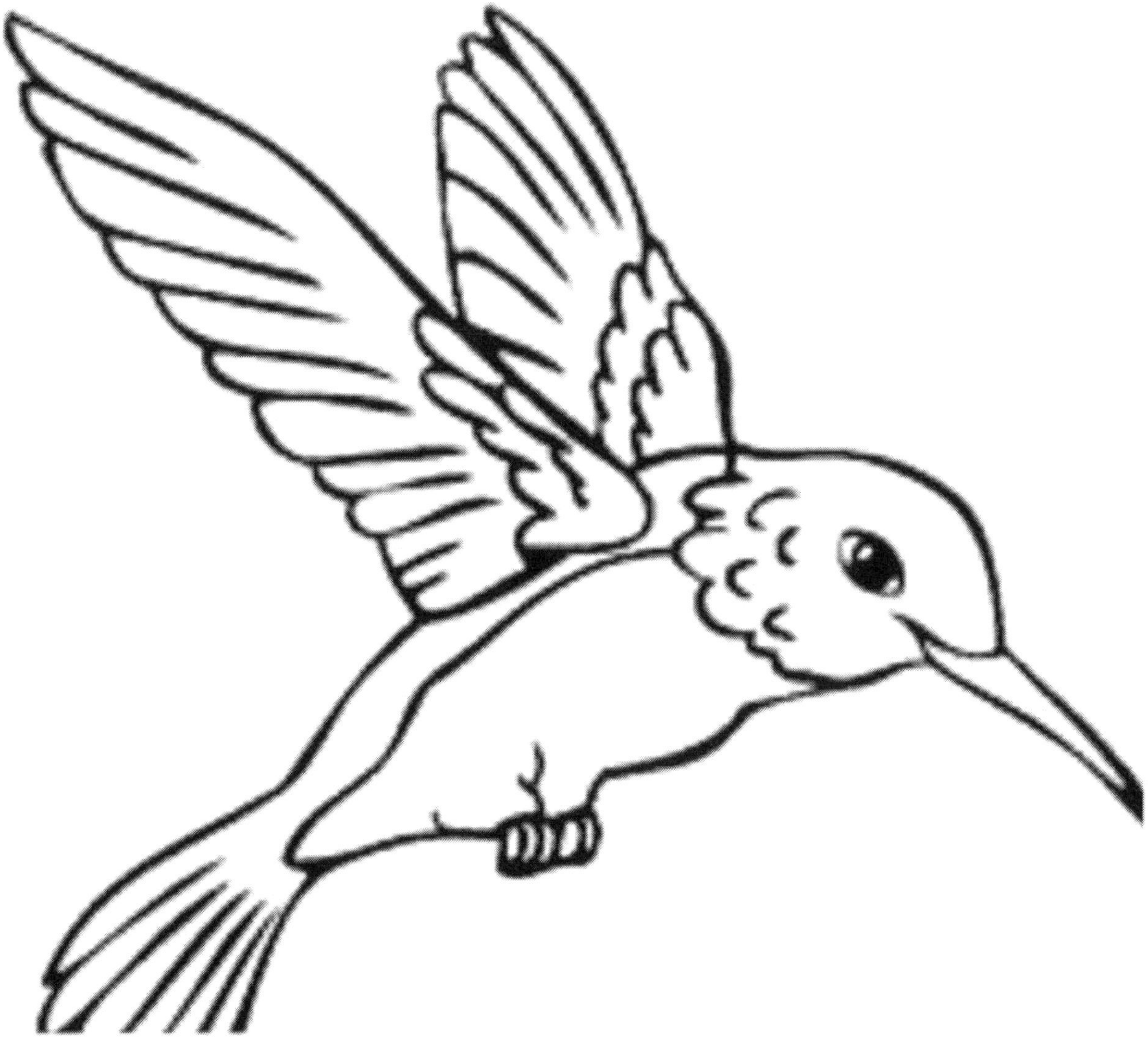

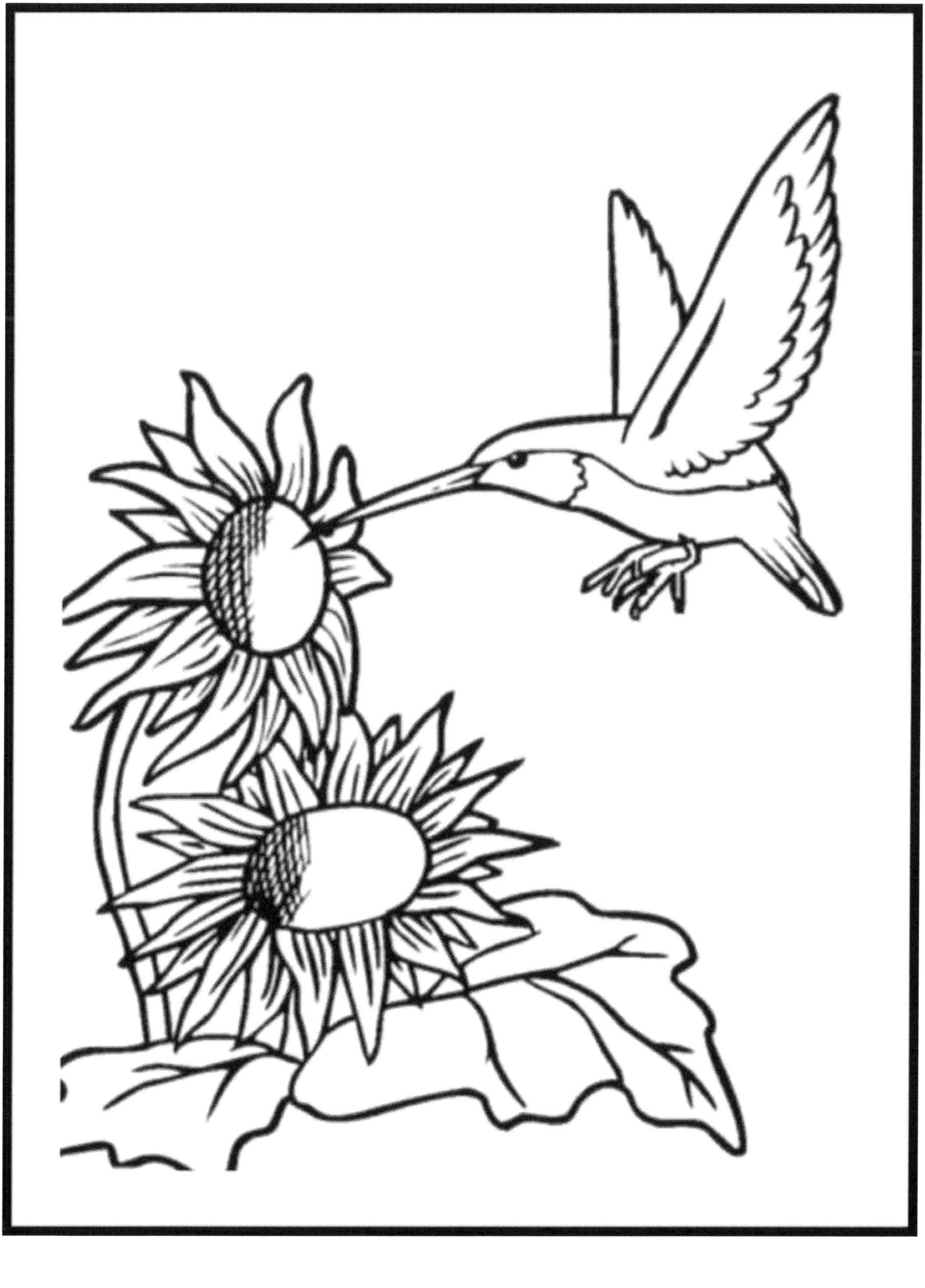

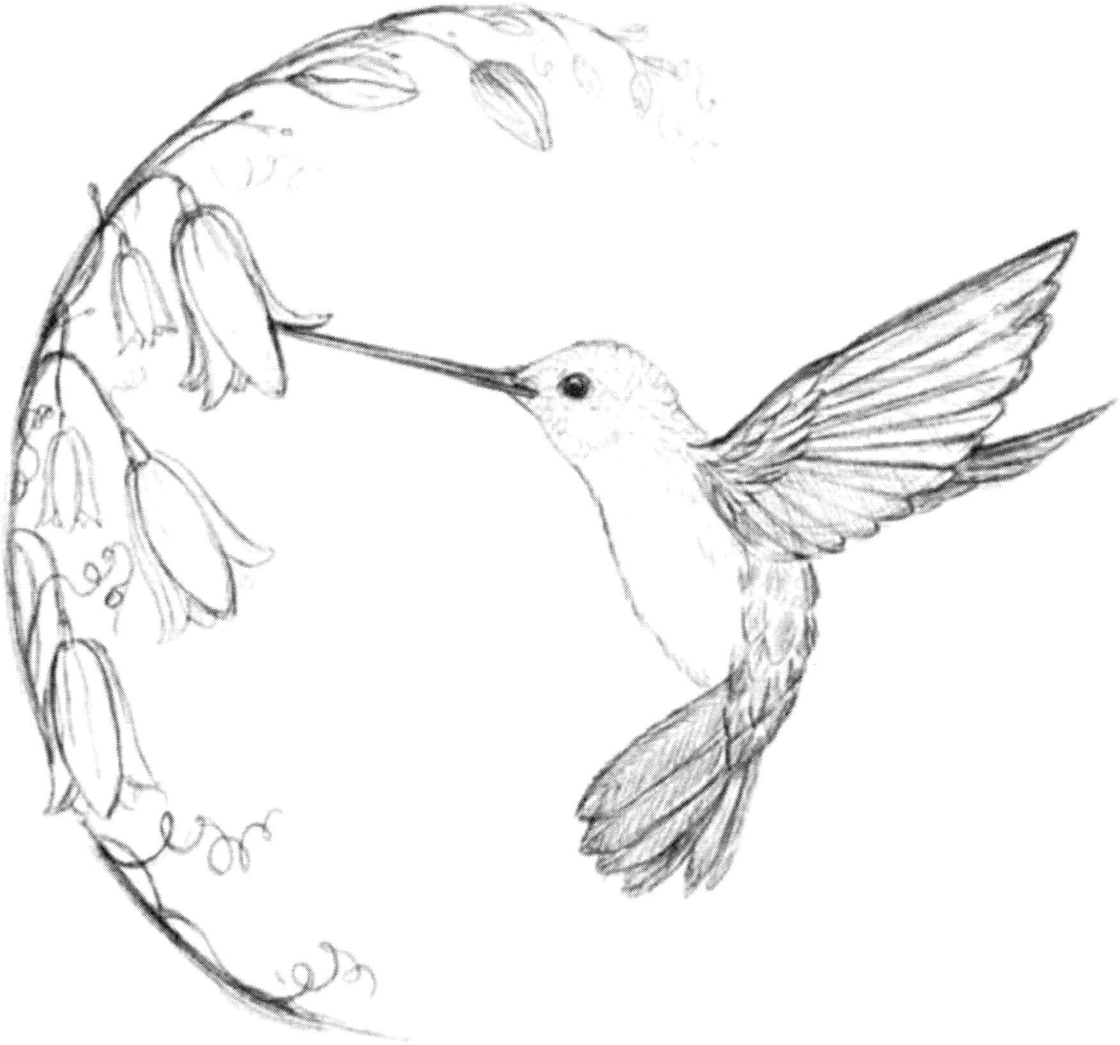

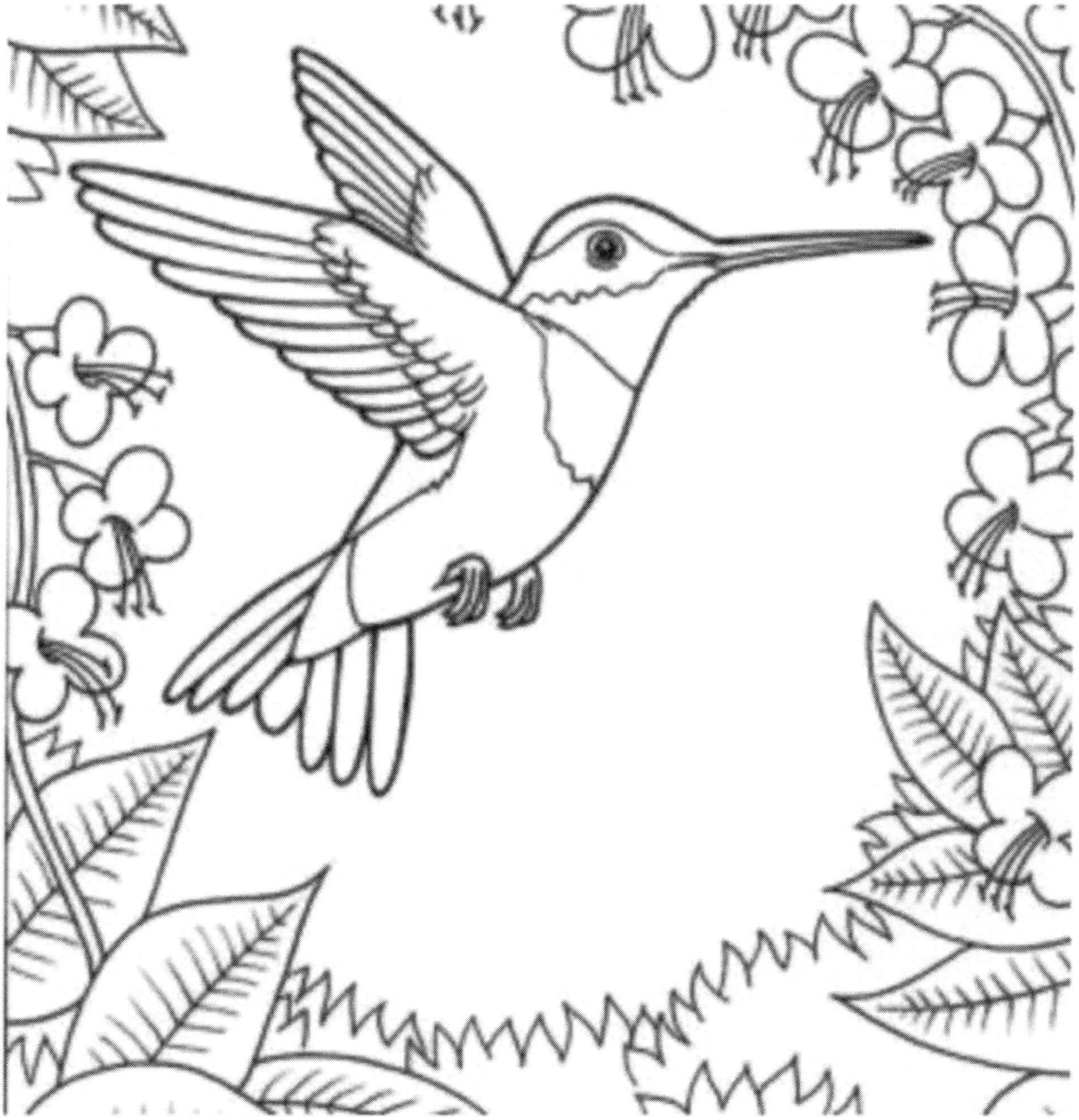

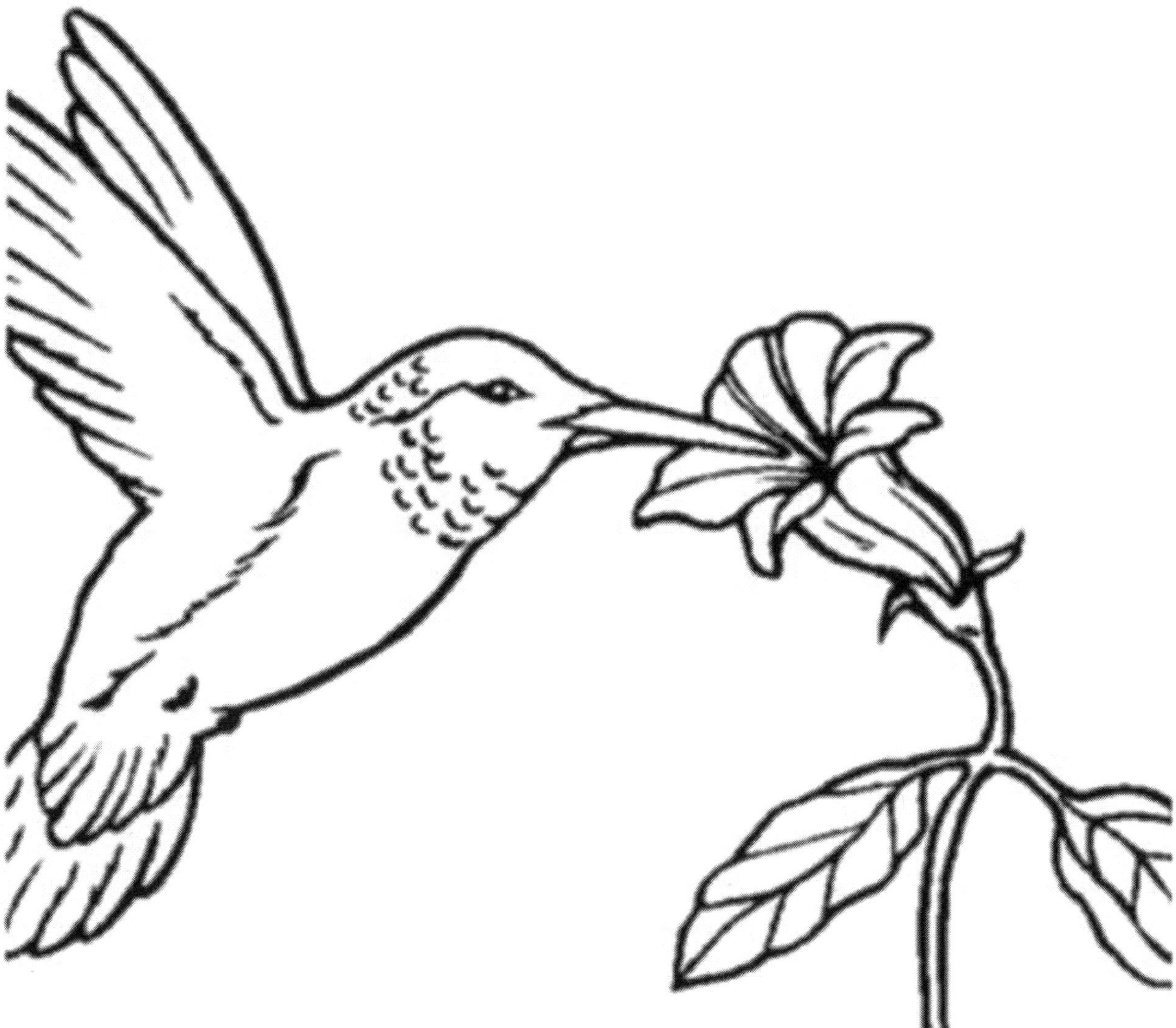

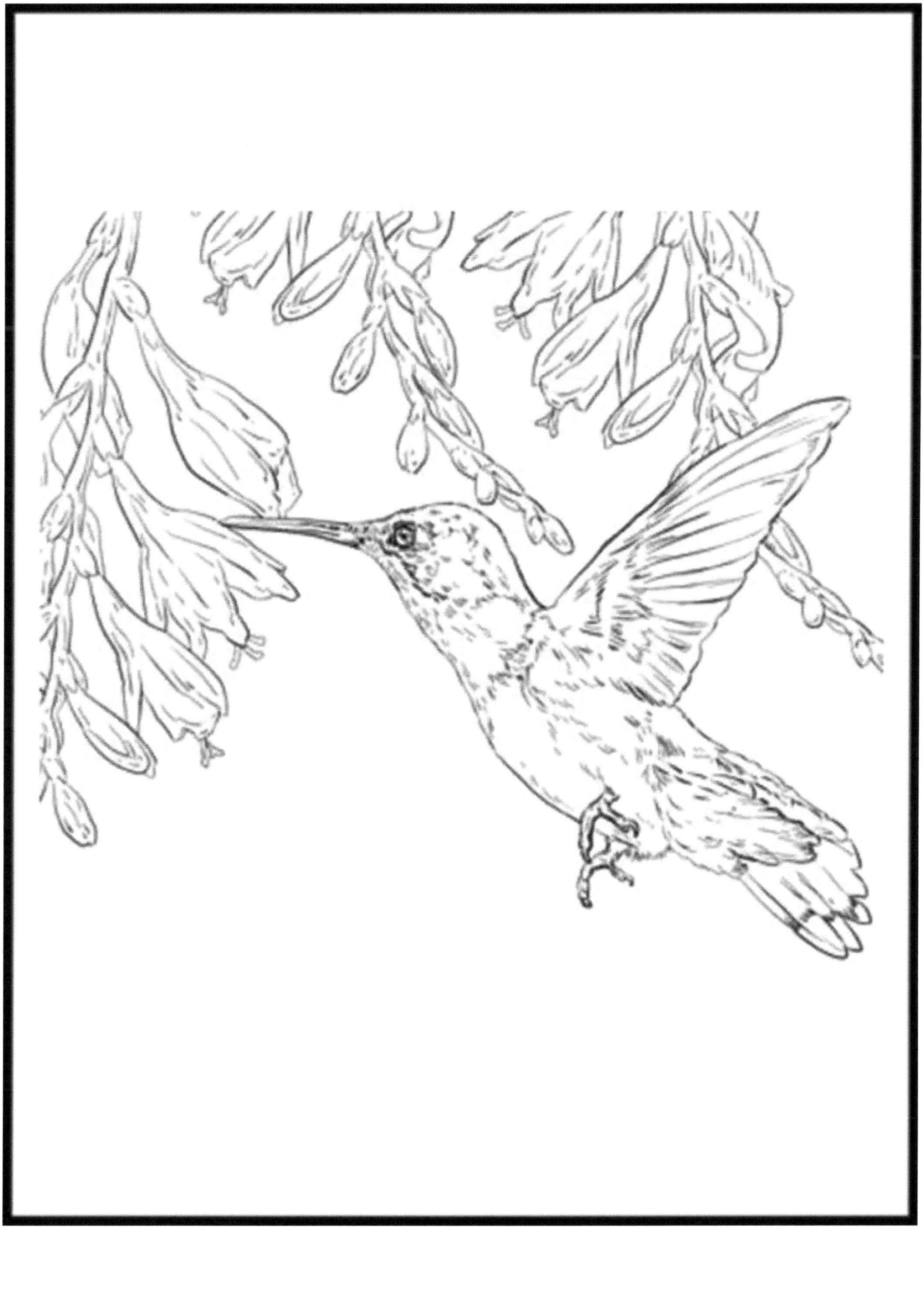

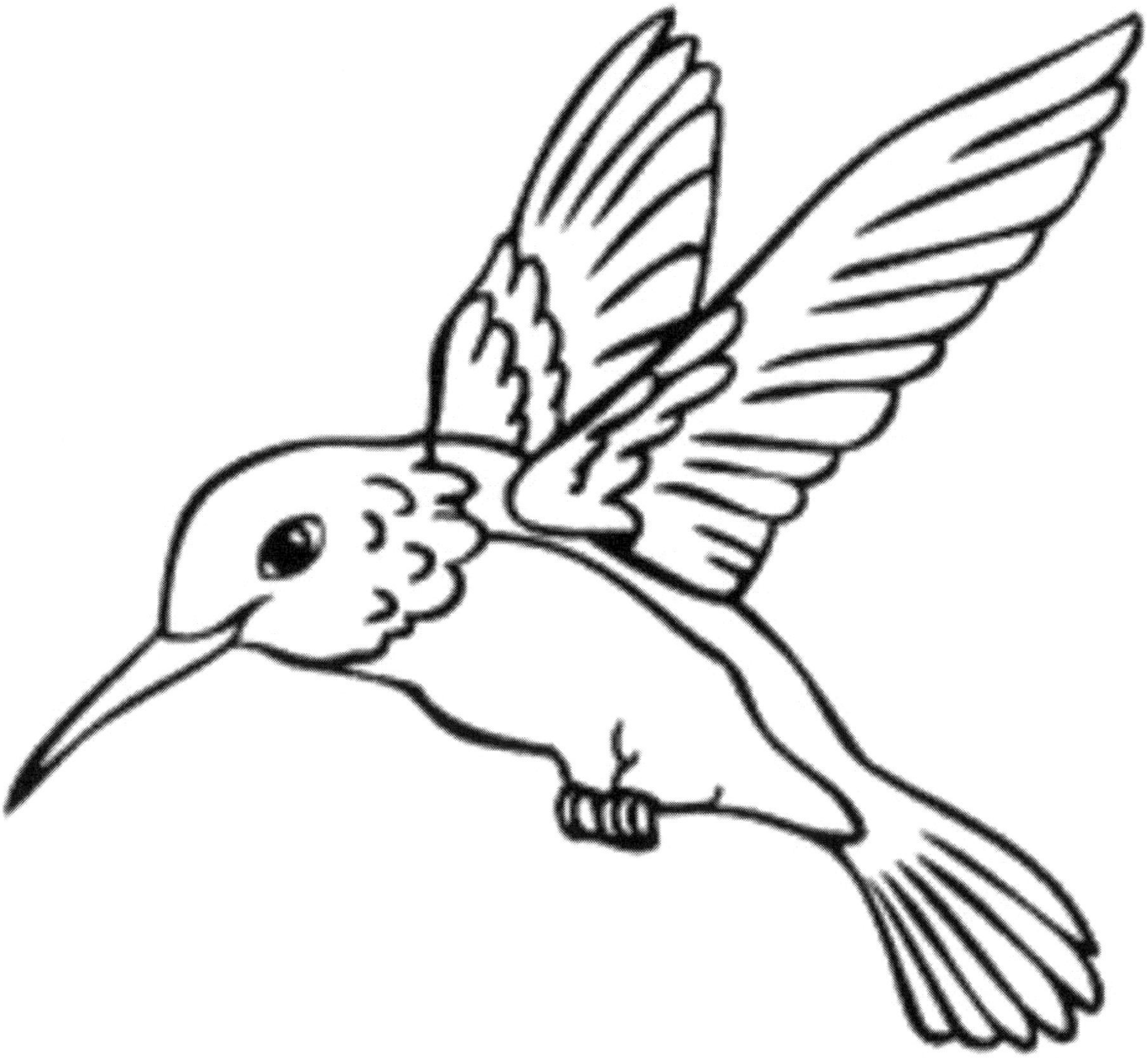

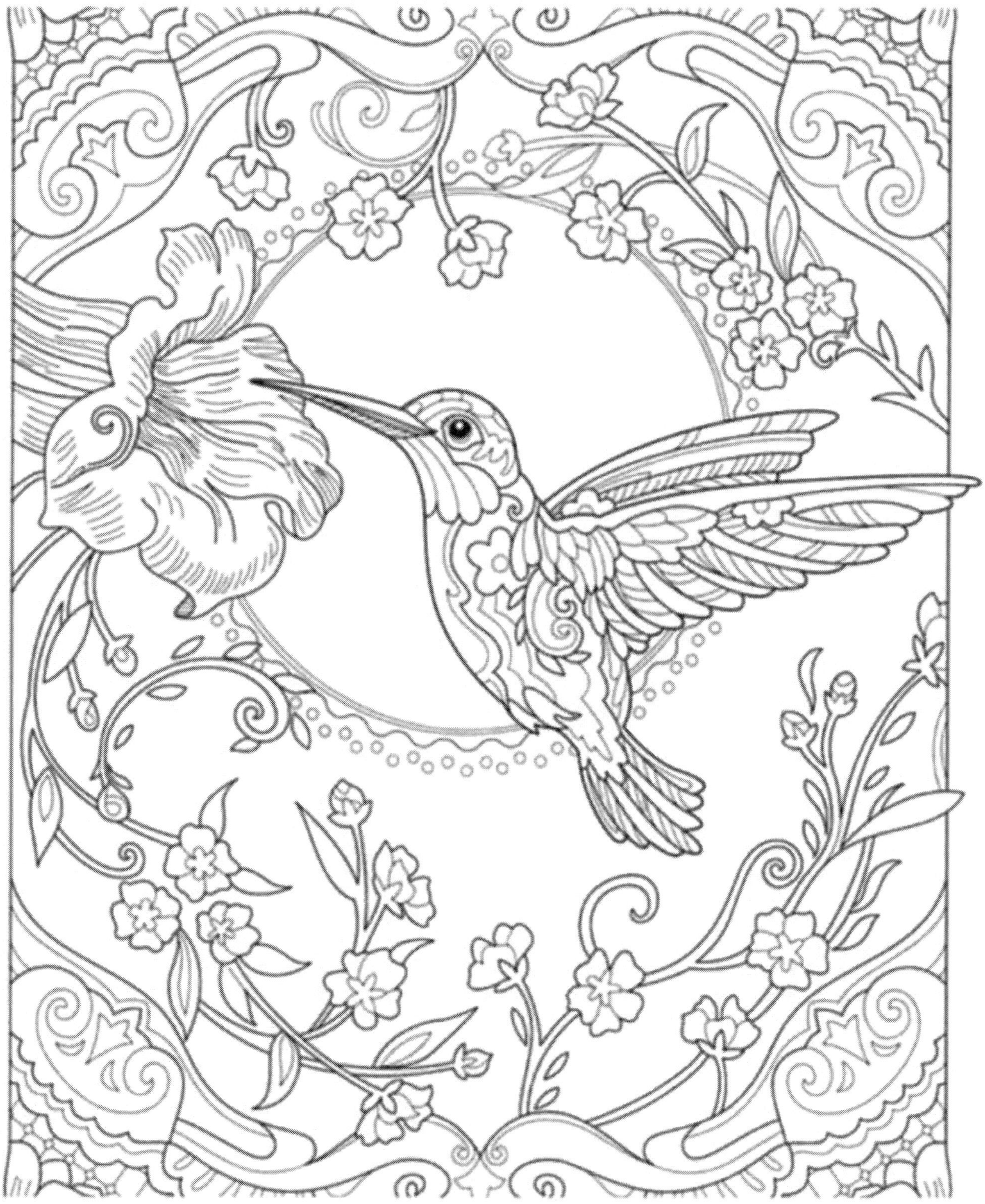

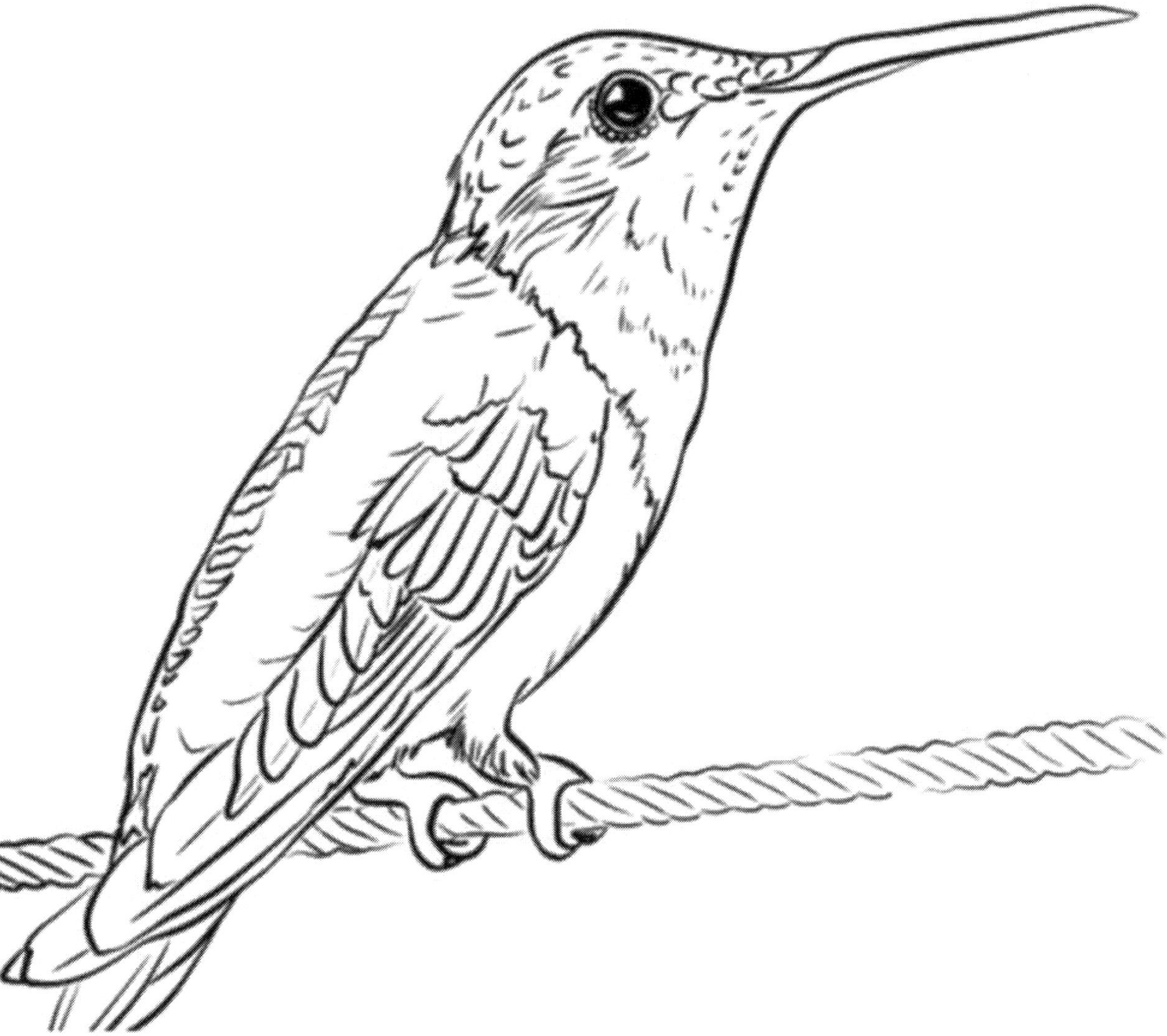

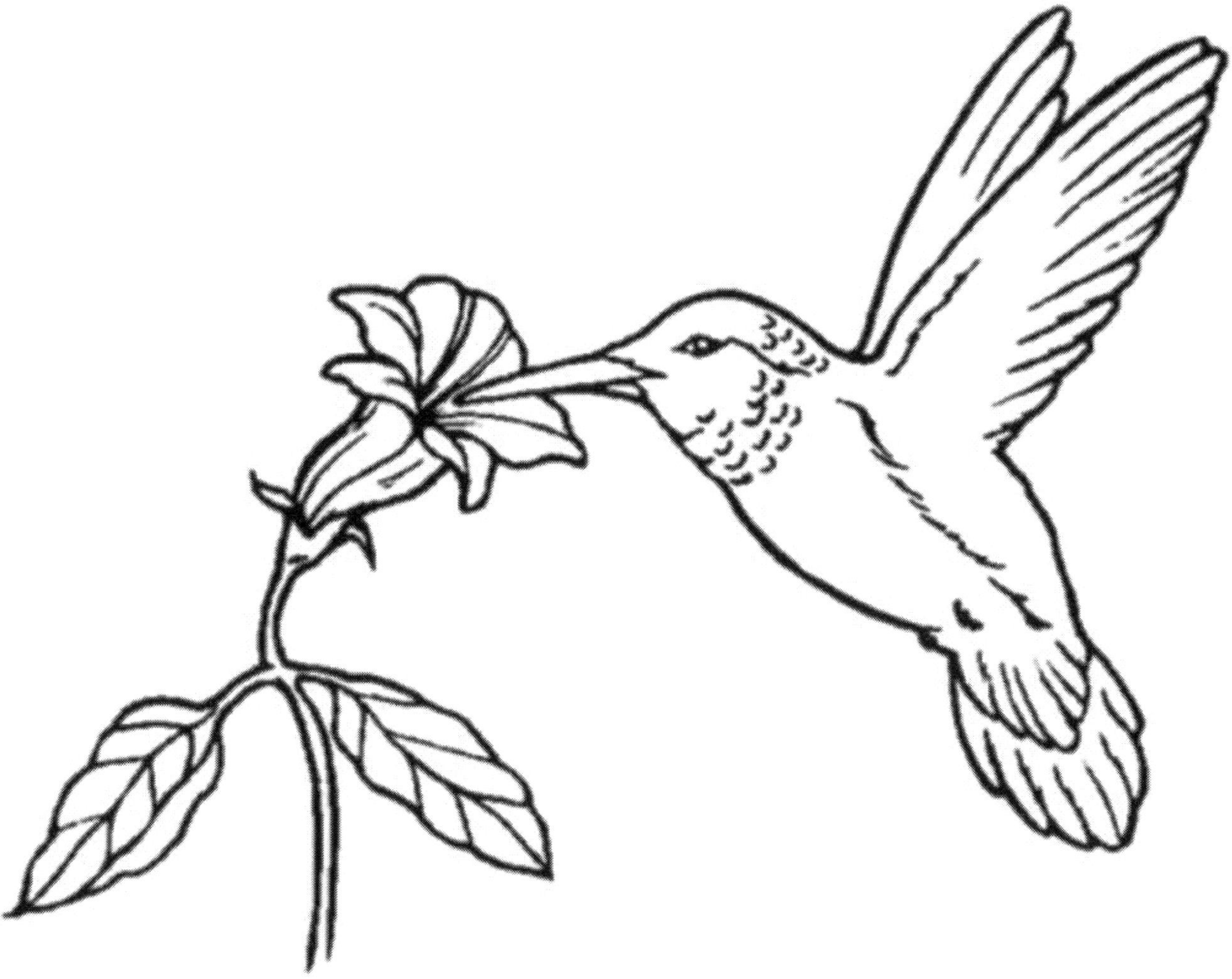

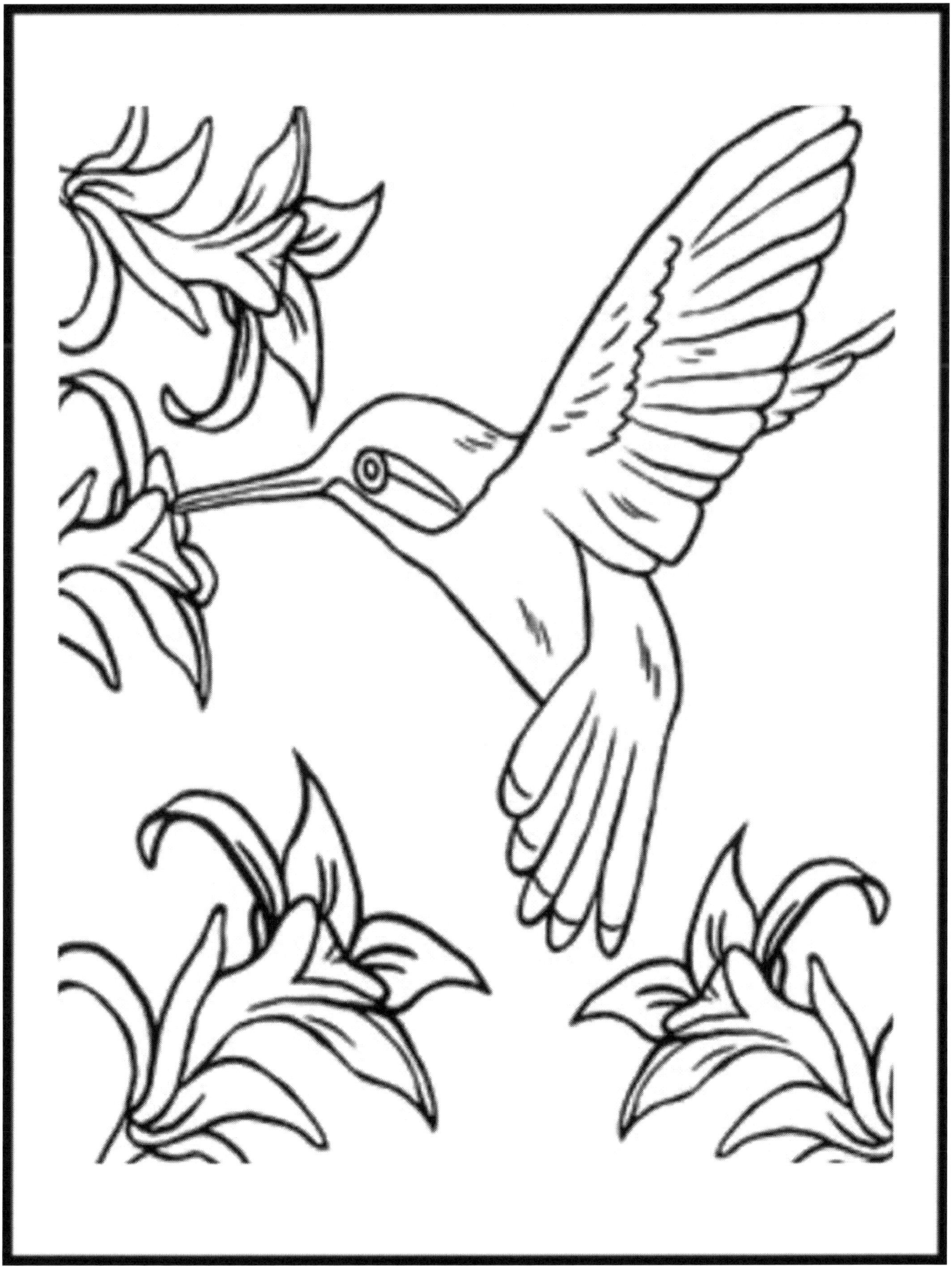

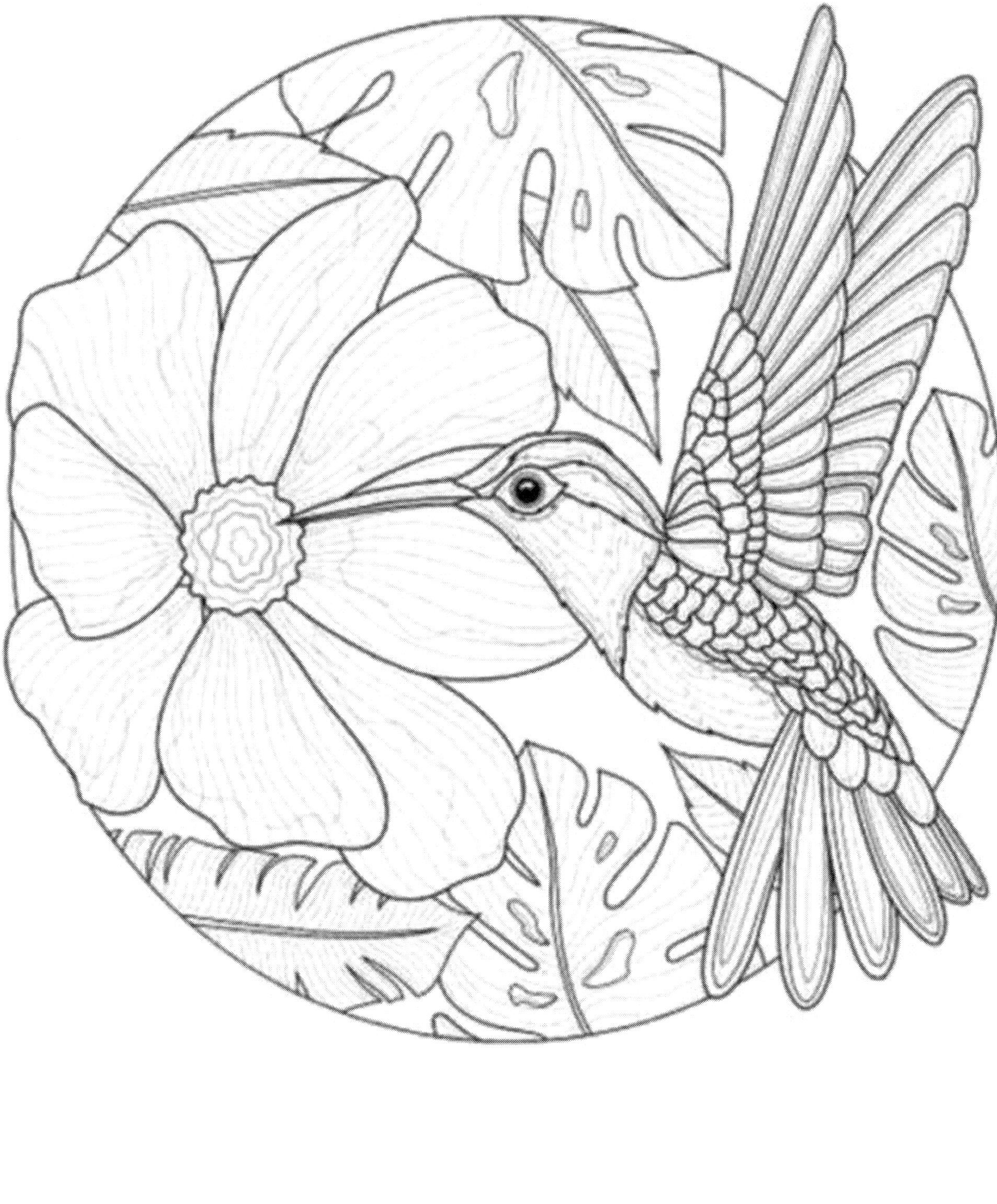

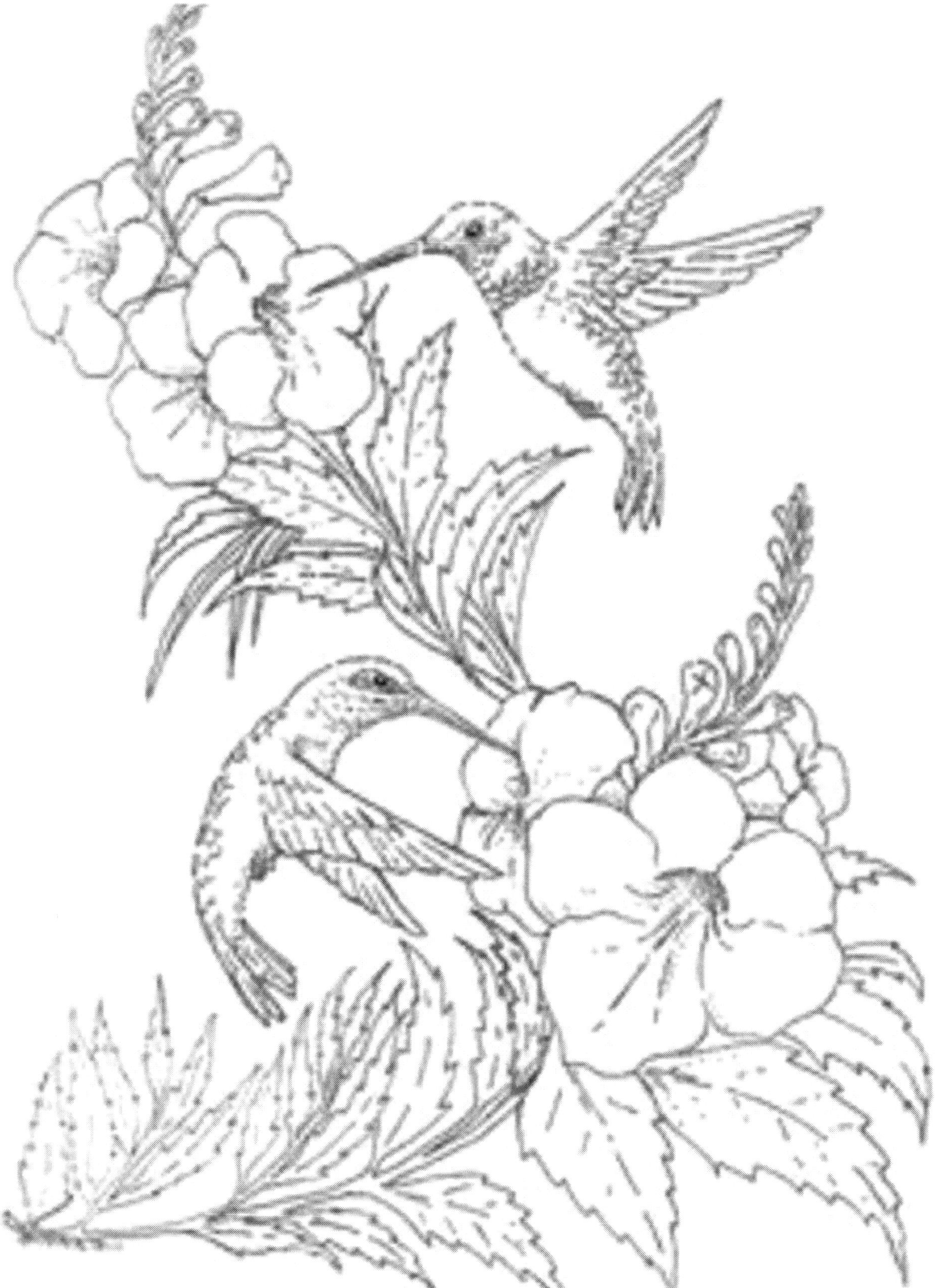

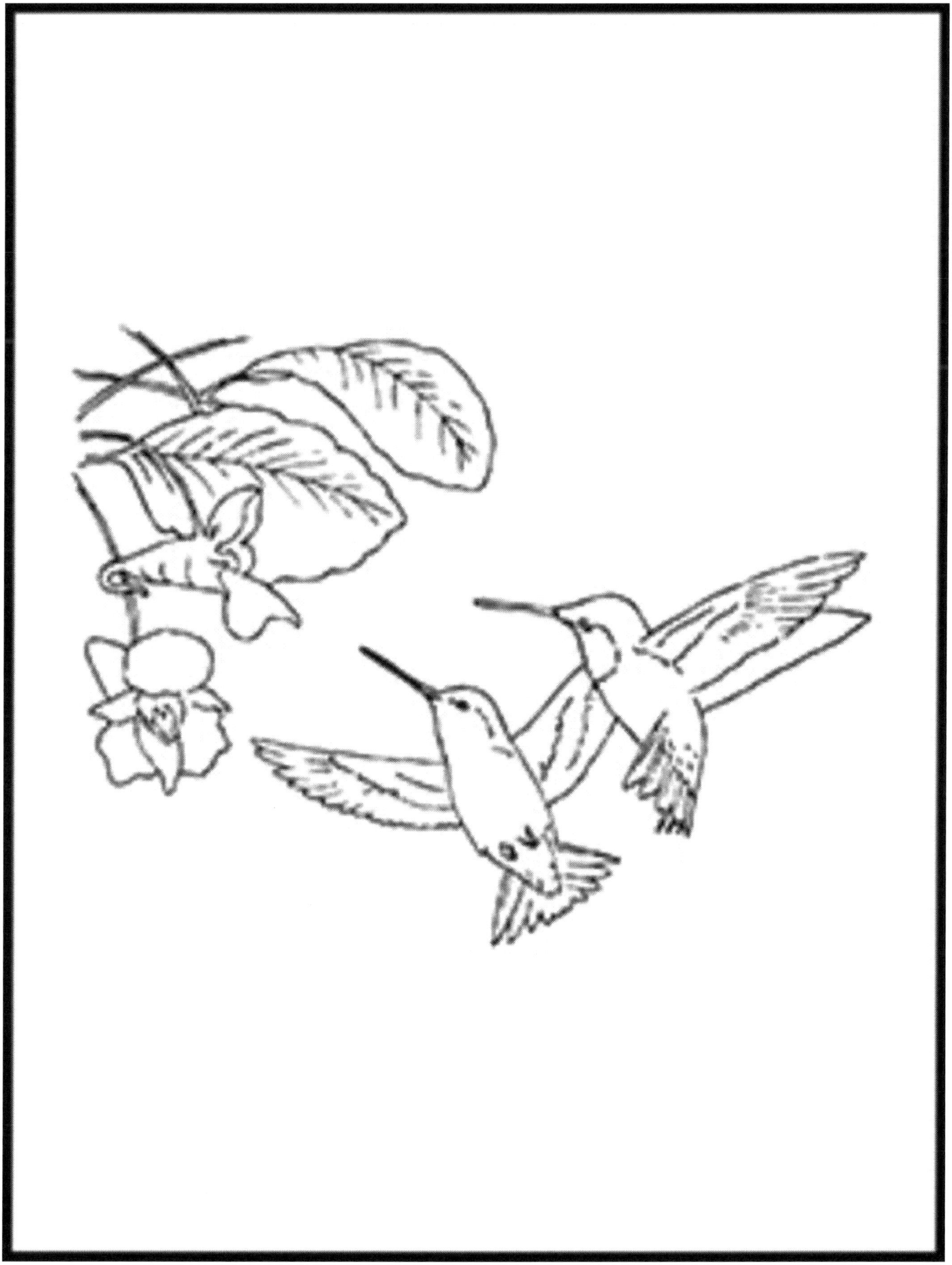

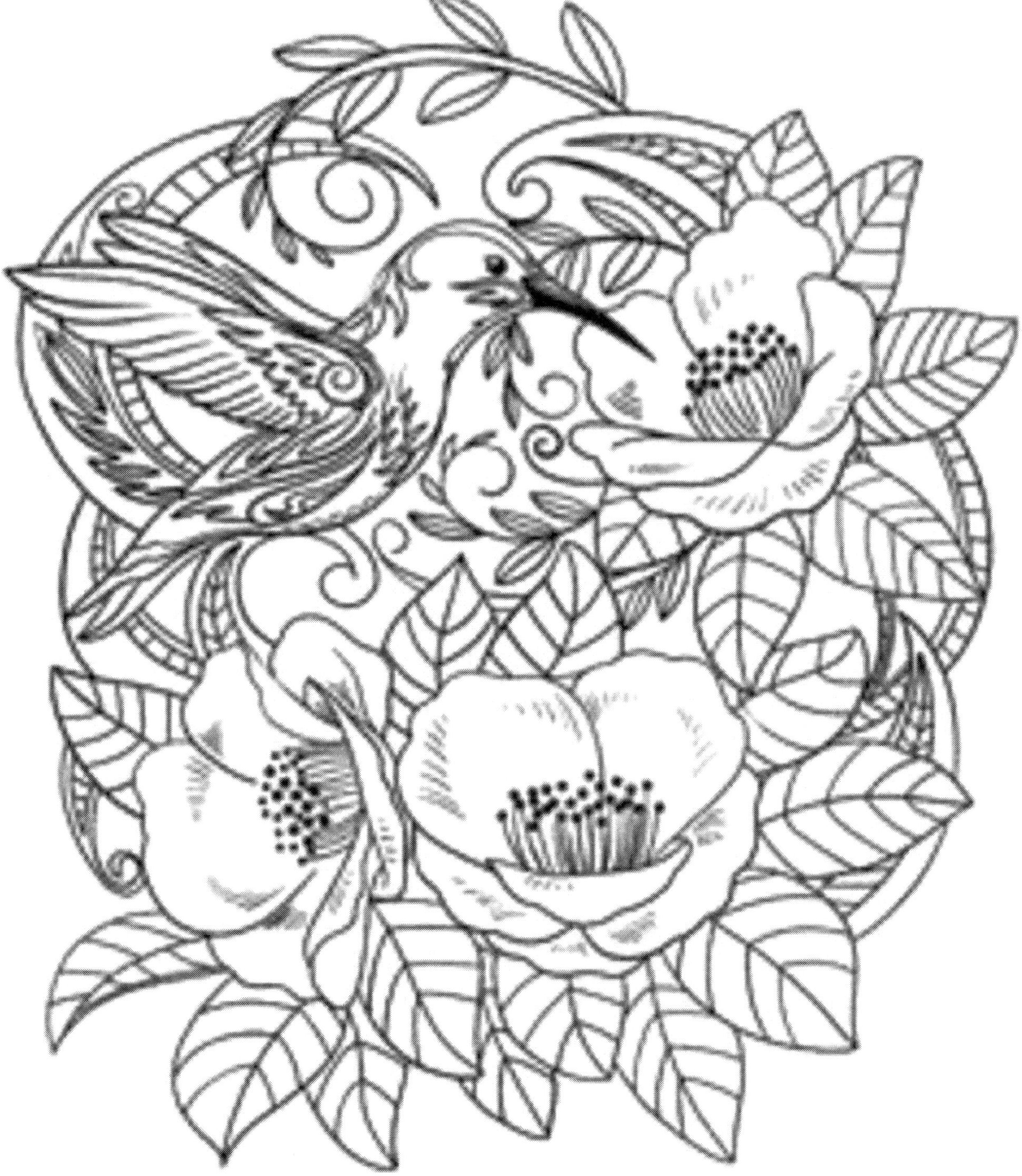

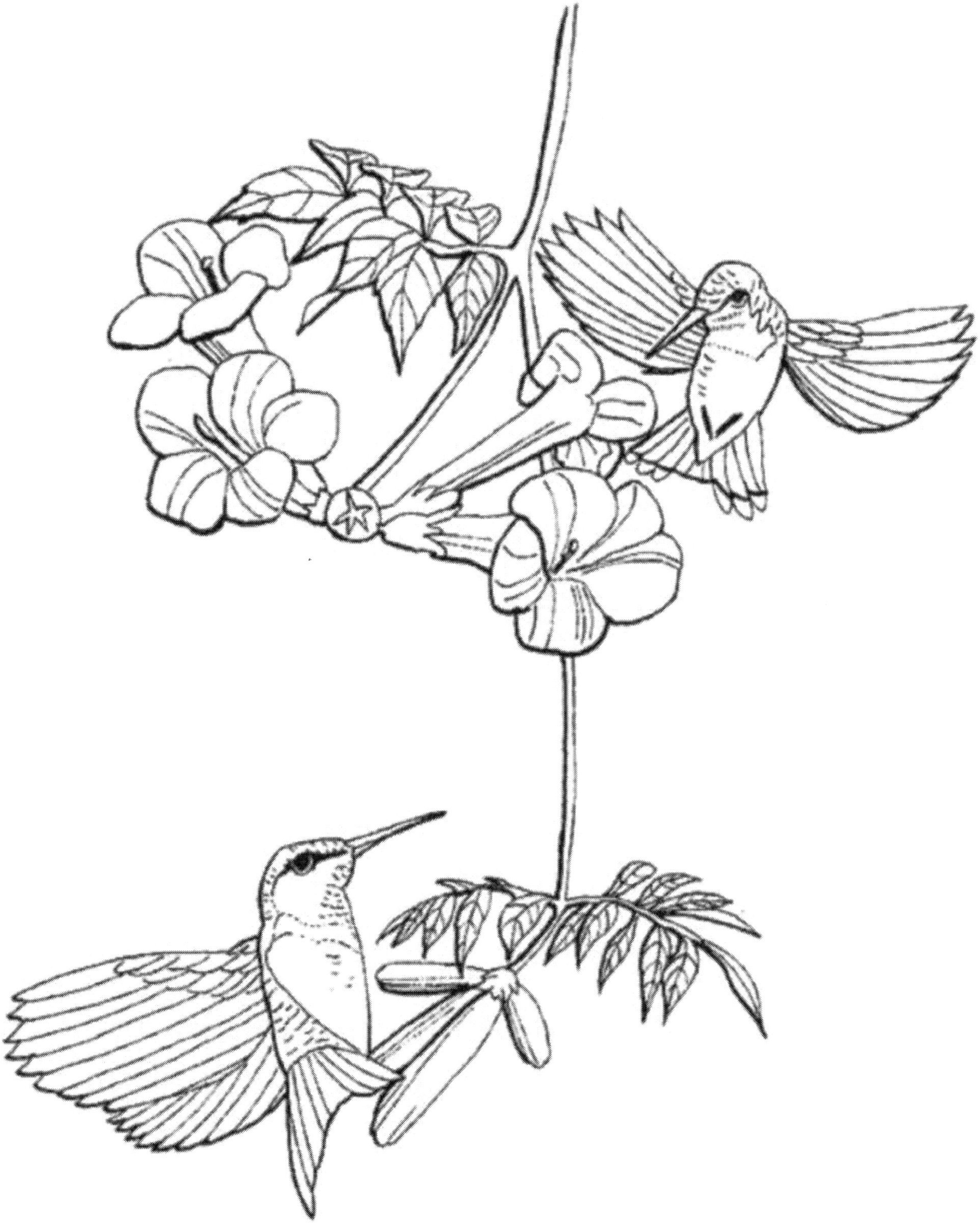

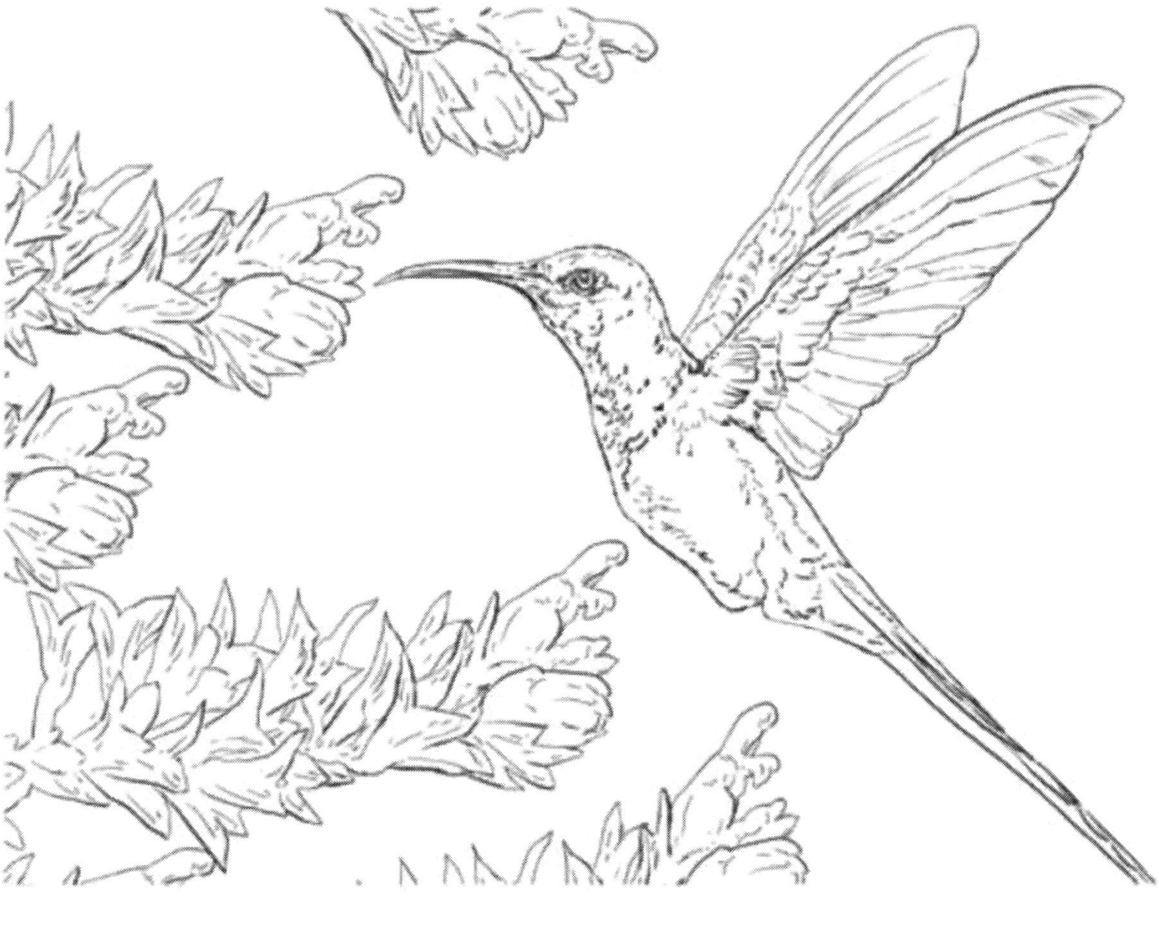

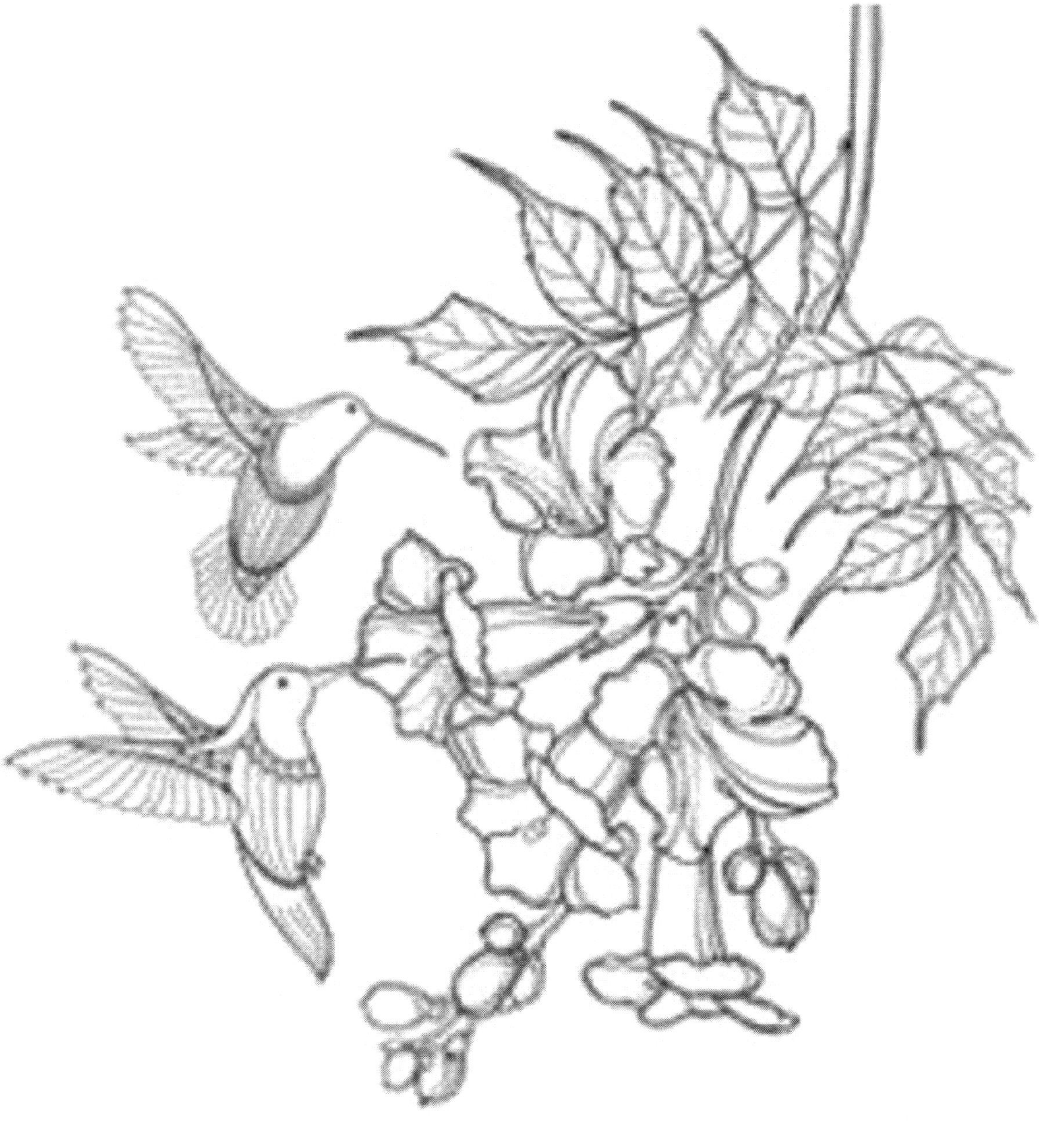

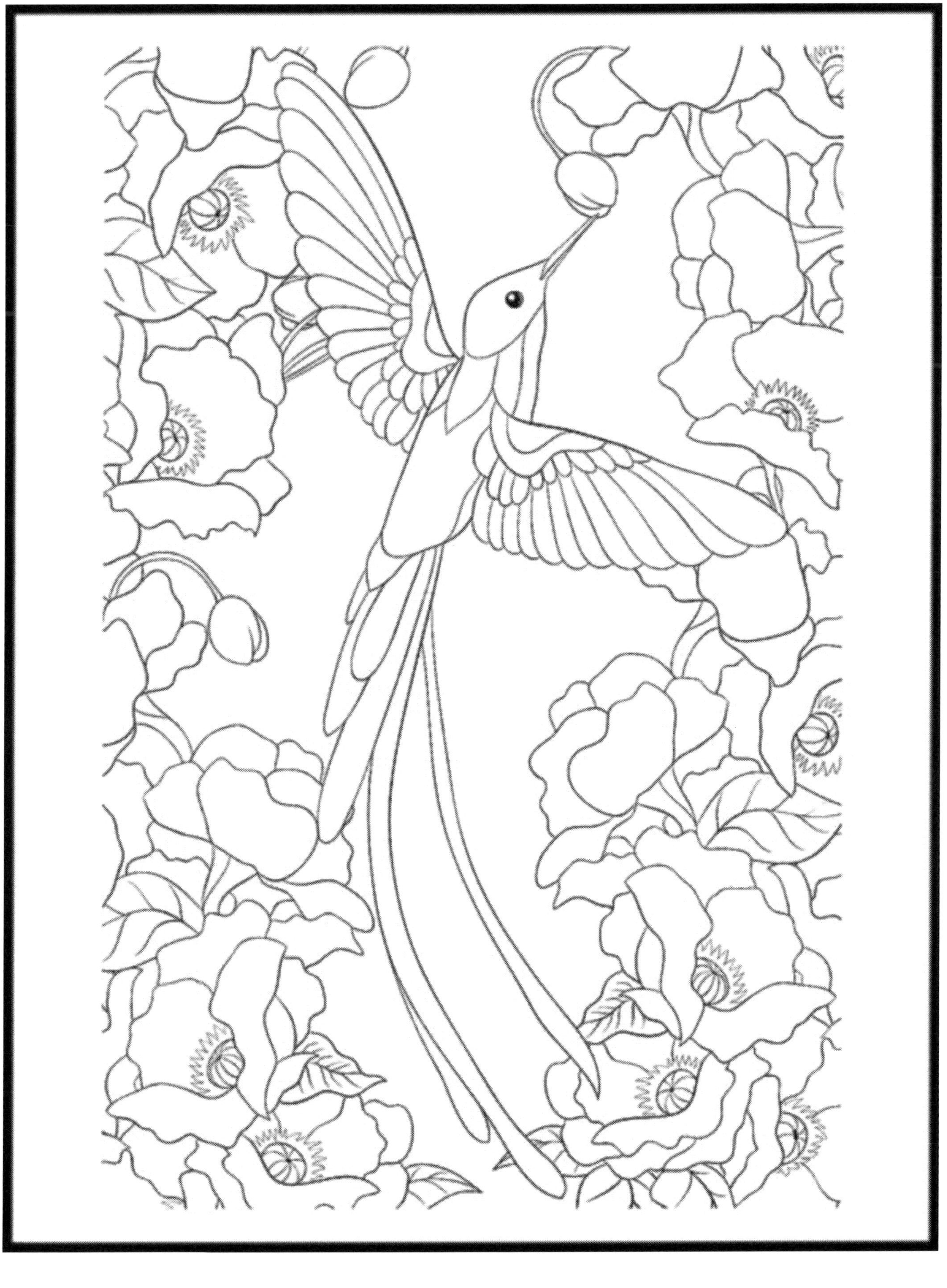

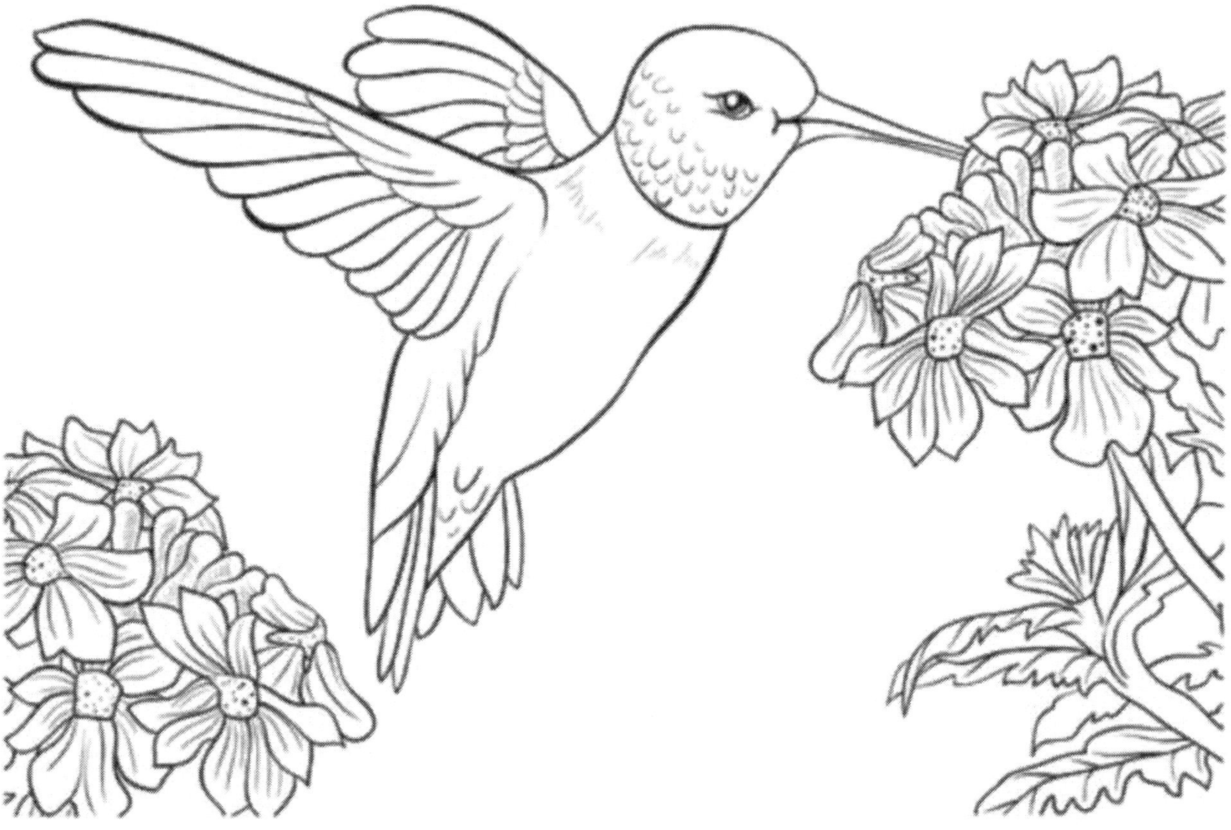

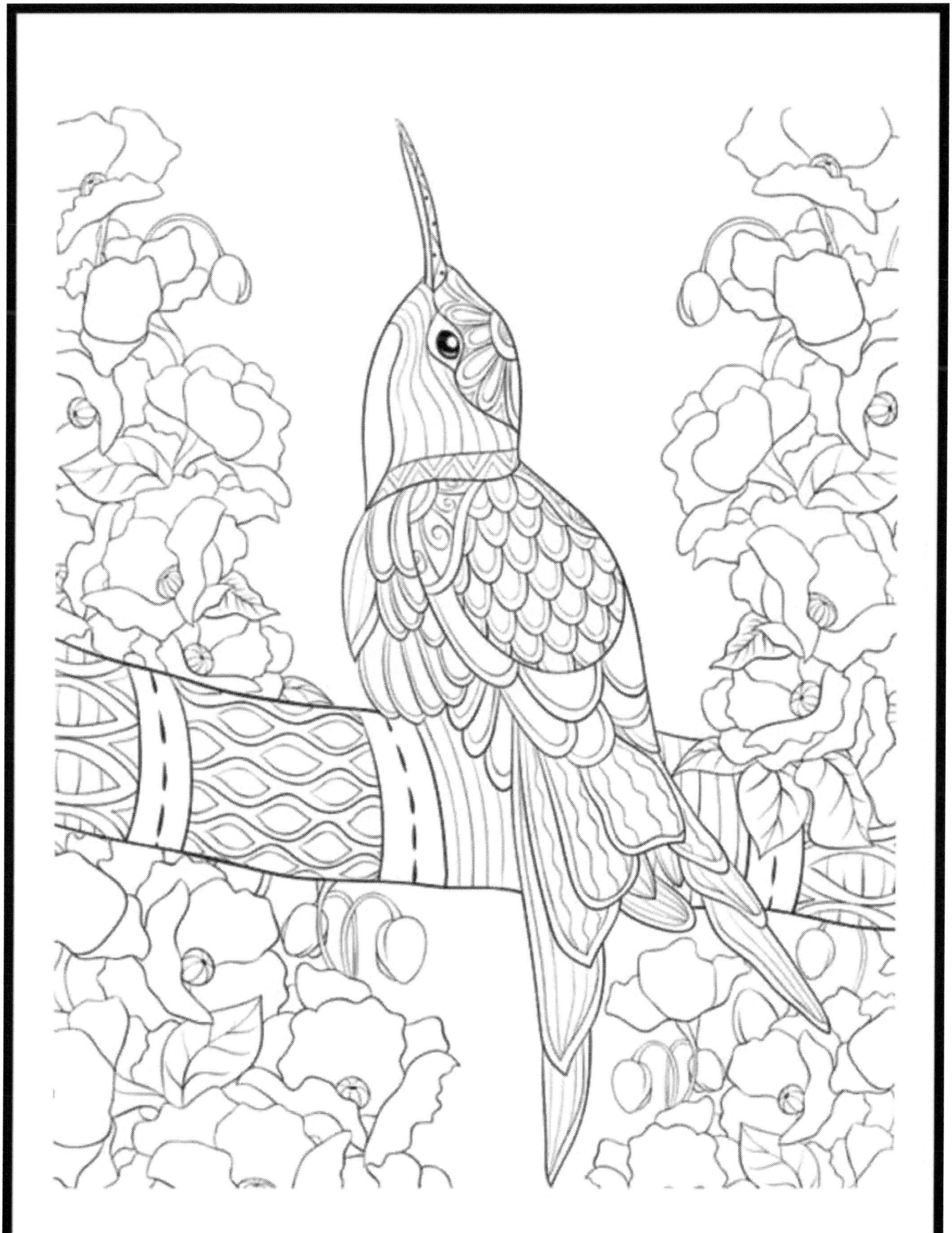

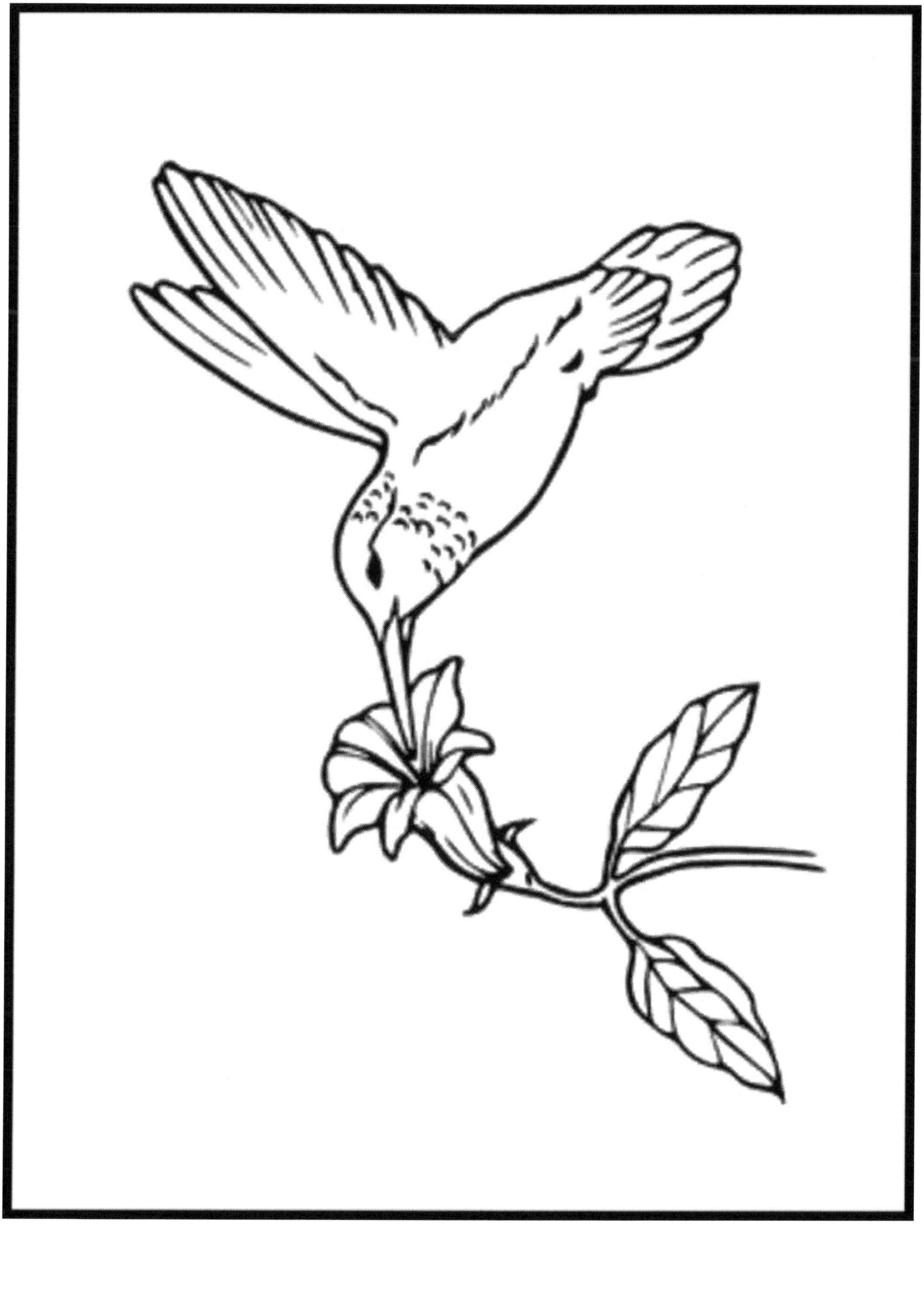

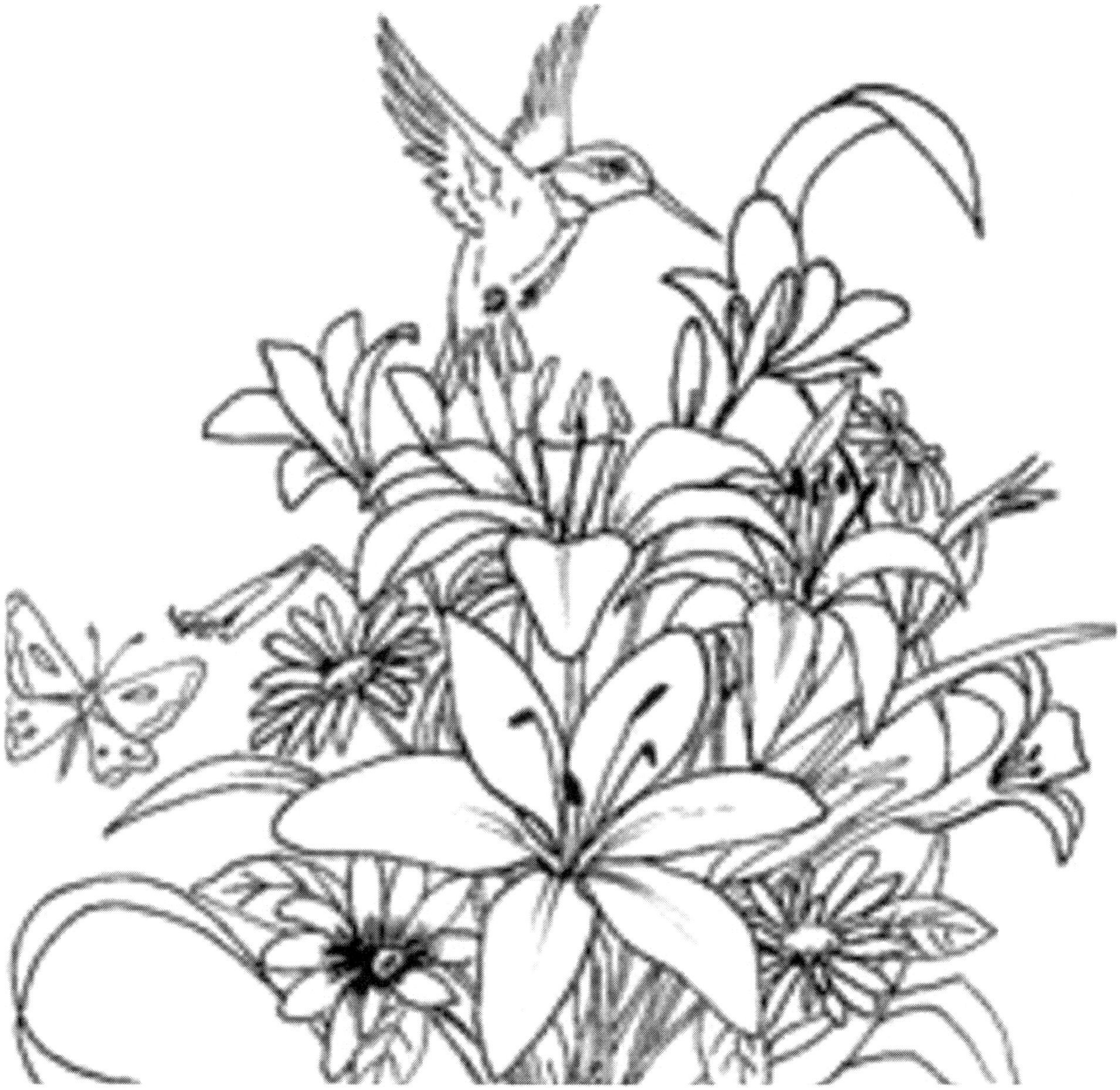

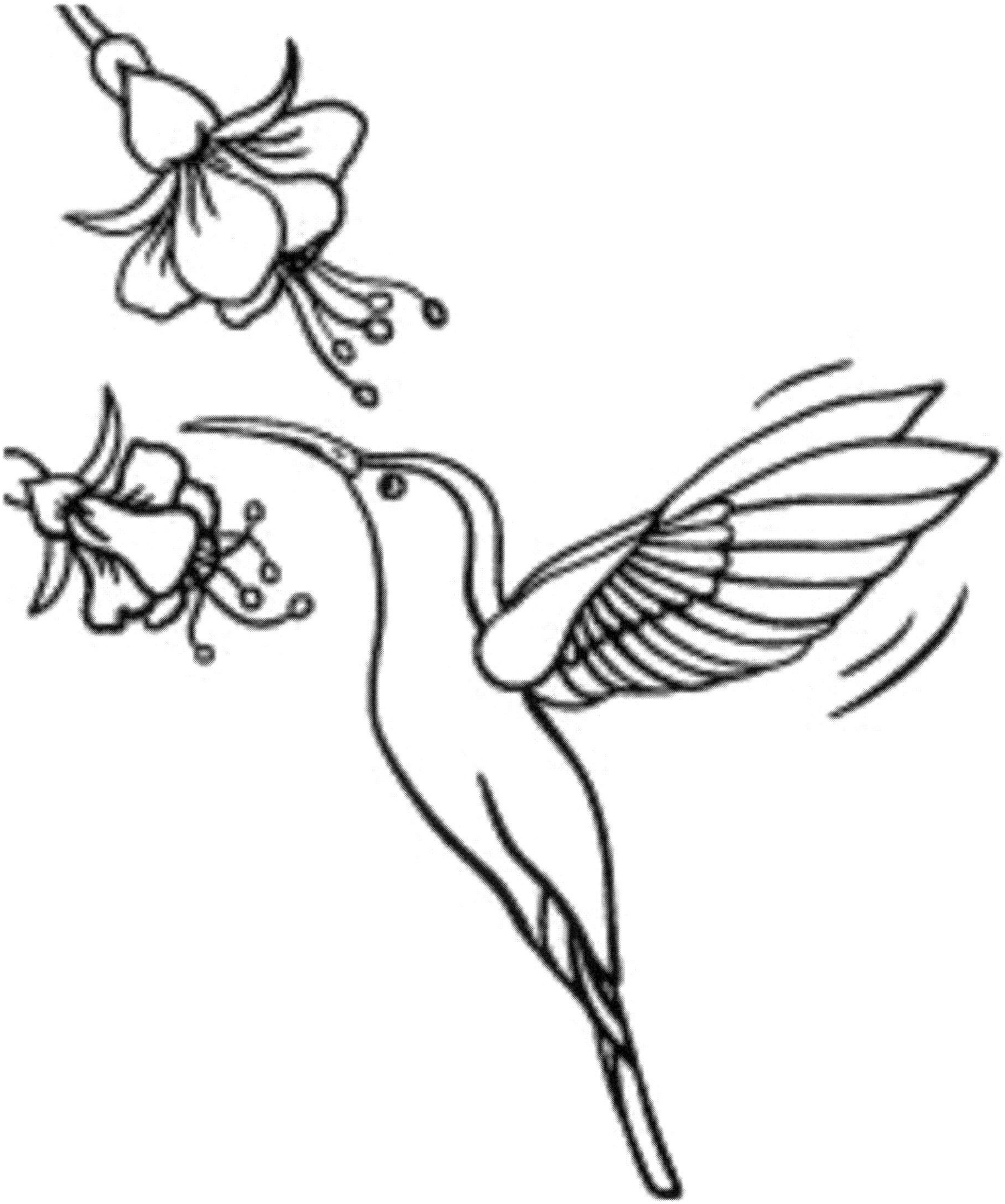

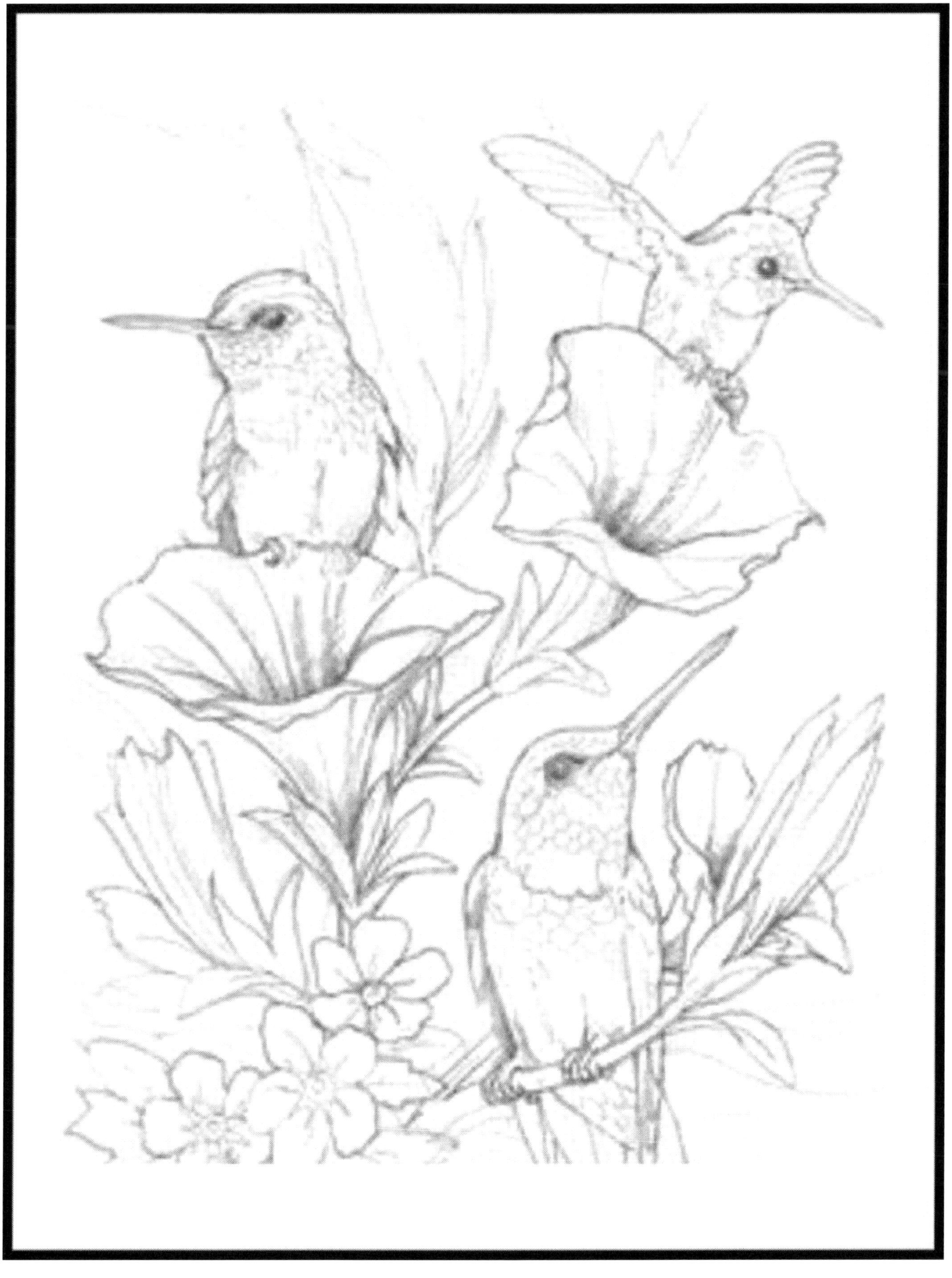

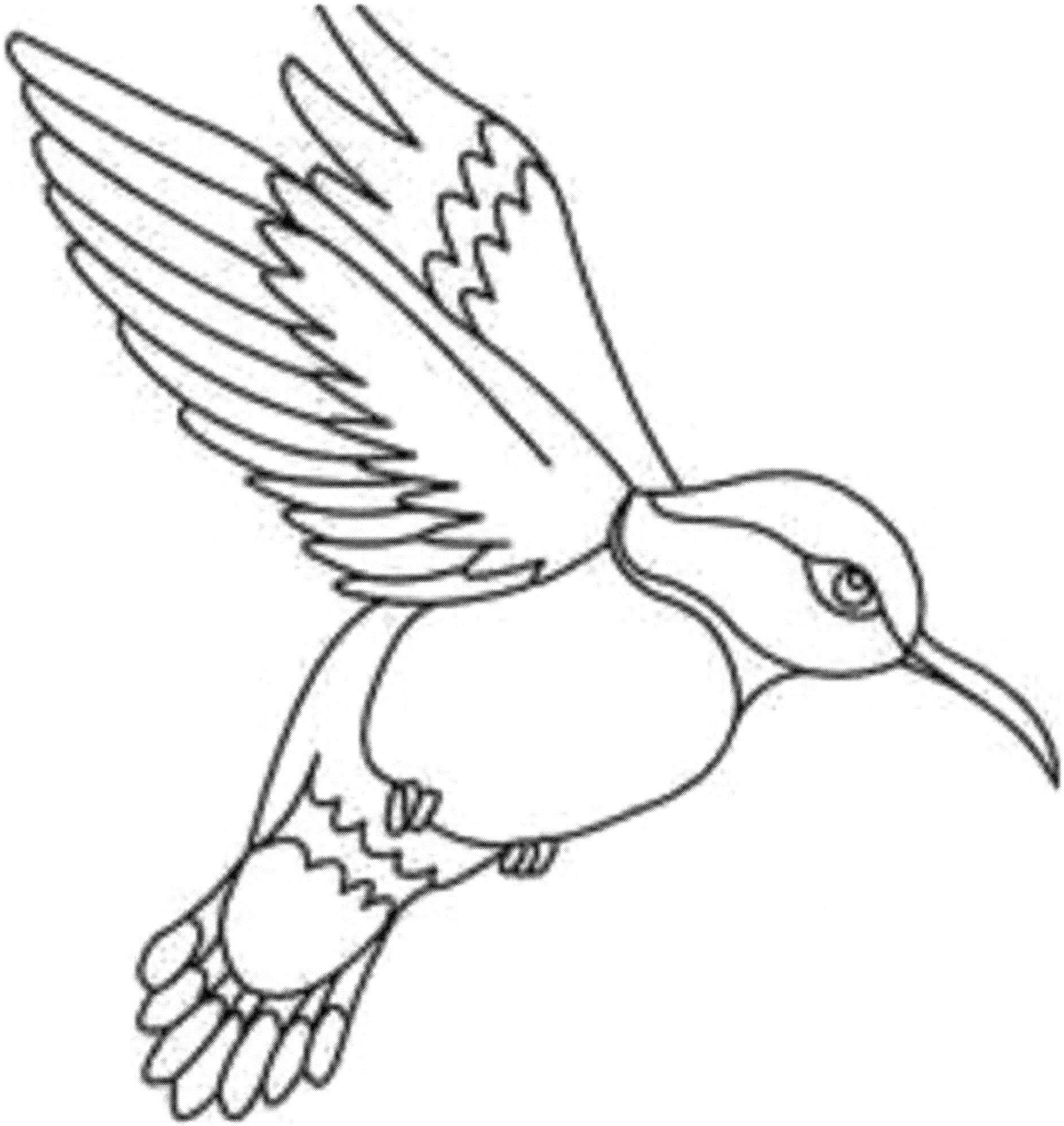

Made in United States
Troutdale, OR
11/10/2023

14456290R00058

Made in United States
Troutdale, OR
11/10/2023

14456290R00058